Teach Us To Pray

A Study of Distinctively Christian Praying

CHARLES FRANCIS WHISTON
Associate Professor of Moral Theology,
Church Divinity School of the Pacific,
Berkeley, California

With an Introduction by

NELS F. S. FERRÉ
Abbot Professor of Christian Theology,
The Andover Newton Theological School,
Newton Centre, Massachusetts

WIPF & STOCK · Eugene, Oregon

Wipf and Stock Publishers
199 W 8th Ave, Suite 3
Eugene, OR 97401

Teach Us to Pray
A Study of Distinctively Christian Praying
By Whiston, Charles Francis
Copyright© January, 1949 by Pilgrim Press
ISBN 13: 978-1-60899-174-7
Print date: March 2003
Previously published by Pilgrim Press, 1949

This book is dedicated to
God
as a thank offering for
Estelle, my wife,
through whom I have been
taught so deeply
of the love of God

Contents

The Power of Prayer	Nels F. S. Ferré	vii

PART I THE VISION

Chapter
1. Teach Us to Pray 3

PART II "FOUNDED UPON A ROCK"

2. The Initiative of God 21
   Creator and Creature 25
3. Immortality or Eternal Life by Resurrection? 35
   Redeemer and Redeemed . . . 39
4. The Indwelling Spirit 44
   God — Untempted and Sinless . . 48
5. God's Freedom and Man's . . . 53
   God's Love and Man's . . . 56

PART III "OUR FATHER"

6. Praying as Adoration 65
7. Praying as Adoration (*Continued*) . 81
8. Praying as Self-Giving 95

CONTENTS

9 Praying as Intercession 115
10 Praying as Thankfulness . . . 136

PART IV "DELIVER US"

11 Devotional Reading 147
12 Temptation and Praying . . . 168
13 Sin, Forgiveness and Praying . . . 180
14 Perseverance 189

PART V "FOR THEIR SAKES"

15 The Retreat 201
16 The School of Prayer 212
17 The Layman's Life of Praying . . 221
18 The Minister's Life of Praying . . 226

PART VI "EXCEPT YE BE CONVERTED"

19 Praying and Social Issues . . . 241

The Power of Prayer

NOT TO RECOGNIZE and to face the seriousness of our times is heedlessly to court disaster. Our days are dark with death and the future seems frozen with terror. With most people who are aware of our actual situation, depth-dark forebodings are shot through with only minor, or occasional, streaks of hope. Yet the deeper truth still is that man's permanent predicament is at a time like this made all the more clear. Even while we live in a constantly precarious environment, all of us are ever on the swift march to death. Quiet comfort and apparent social and political security are temptations to distort, or actually to hide us from, our real situation as we face God and eternity. External insecurity is, at least, the proper occasion for the securing of inner peace through the laying hold of God's eternal promises and the finding of the peace of God which nothing can disturb.

Such peace of mind and heart will also release spiritual dynamic and social creativity. While these are lacking, our social and political conditions must be upset, and if continued, hurl themselves to destruction. Christian disciples should always be the salt of the earth wherewith the earth is salted. They must, as the author of the Epistle to Diognetus said, "hold the world together." Toynbee's Creative Minority it is which keeps both the soul and the body social from disintegrating. Heaven and earth cannot be sundered without doing injury to both. What is right, and the power to effect it, must be determined and come from above. This simply means that the one essential condition both for eternal salvation and for earthly well-being is prayer. Prayer is the mightiest force in the world, for all other forms of power are of earth temporal, but genuine prayer is man's communion with God and his newness of life with his fellow men within that communion. It is, in other words, the very essence of spiritual relations, and they alone are eternal.

Prayer *is light*. God alone is pure light, and only in his light do we see light. All true light is finally from above. The Holy Spirit dispels our darkness and sheds light into our lives by his anointing, the anointing which "teaches us all things, and is truth." The Holy Spirit must lead us into all truth, and that is centrally God's truth in Christ, which alone can make us free from the darkness of self, sin, and death. The natural man lets his self get in between God and the light he needs. He simply shuts it out from his life by turning away from it; only God's grace, therefore, through repentance and through its continually being replenished in prayer, can turn him around and make him open up to the light of life. In the world, too, outside him, the reign of sin has darkened the way the world looks at all things. Not only is the world frail and lacking light because of its own weakness, but, even more, it is sinful, refusing the true light because of its own darkened self-will. All of man's activities and all secular education are consequently mixed darkly gray with sin. The world's wisdom, moreover, is easy to confuse with the best truth available, because it is so commonly accepted. But it is also in abundant measure the foolishness of fear, doubt, and rebellion. Therefore, the person who is to bring light to that world must continually have his vision renewed and his spiritual eyes strengthened through the practice of prayer.

The sinful self also likes to look away from death. Sin incarnate likes to tempt us to think that life is real only here and that eternal life, if any, must somehow be but a part of this life. That assertion shears every spiritual Samson of his hair and makes him too feeble to resist his enemies and to shake the pillars of evil. Prayer, on the other hand, puts us in the focus of the true light, the light which is indescribably beyond this life, and yet also truly here, for us all, even now. Prayer, when right with God, places us in the perspective of light and power.

For prayer *is power*. All power is of God. The power to do evil is permissive only, and merely temporary for the sake of our freedom. Prayer, when proper, is the power for good, God's good for each and for the whole world. The constant refrain of Jesus was that faith was power. Faith is nothing but our affirmation in communion with God of his never-failing love, however expressed. Faith is power for freedom and fellowship obtained through the process of prayer. For prayer is the constant communion with God through which we learn to trust him. Through prayer the love of God, and ours for him, become increasingly real. Through the power of God, after nights of prayer, Jesus cast out the demons. Some, even, would not go out without prayer and fasting. When Jesus was gone from them, the disciples wisely and obediently waited in prayer, until they should be filled with power from on high. Today again, and perhaps particularly, we need that prayer and that power from on high. Life is a matter of choices among conflicting powers. Our little wills have in themselves no power to save or to change the world, not even to escape for ourselves the powers of evil, within and without. Yet each of us is given the incredible power to change lives and to change the world, when we, by believing in prayer, and in lives such "that our prayers be not hindered," pull open the sluice gate to God's merciful will for the world. In a world slowly disintegrating for lack of moral and spiritual power, or hastening to its own destruction through the demonic use of the power it has acquired, we need the fullest possible measure of the creative and directive power and light of prayer.

Only through love can that light and that power come. There is no other way, for God is love, and he who dwells with God dwells in love, else is he a liar. The world is starving for lack of genuine love. Human relations, from family to world relations, crumble for want of it. It simply is not true, and never has been, that any realm of life can get along on the diet of mere power or mere justice. The idea of power politics is all too true, but beyond a certain point of possible perversion of community, the concept is a false abstraction. Where there is no good will there is sheer darkness, for love alone is light. In any community there must be some positive common relation of ideals and interests, some urge of friendship, some fellowship of outlook. No nation can completely smother prayer; often where public worship has been prohibited, and the saints persecuted, from countless shut chambers and from the deep recesses of the hidden heart there have risen the prayers that are answered in God's way in history, and *shall be answered*. Genuine love, steady, rich, creative, and redemptive, is not ours by nature. That is a living relation from God to men. The individual that would be made whole and effective for the world through the light and power of love has to get these through prayer as he humbly and receptively walks with God. The family that would be serene, secure, and effectively contributing to the remaking of the world has to get its healing and binding love through prayer. The church group that would become an example of the kind of community which the world craves, even though usually without knowing what it wants, can become one and strong only in the Lord's love through prayer. Prayer is the answer, and more and more people begin to grasp this fact.

But they need to be taught concretely how to pray. An outstanding teacher of religion recently told me that he had to go to a Hindu swami in order to get concrete suggestions on how to pray. This teacher of philosophy and religion felt that our most crying need is prayer, and yet he could not find the help he needed from the ministers whom he asked to help him. Multitudes of people are joining with the disciples in asking "Teach us to pray." If the spiritual, intellectual, moral, social, and political climate of our day is to be radically reconstituted, we need prayer, prayer by individuals, prayer by living cells, prayer throughout the whole world. Yet what and how shall we pray? *Teach us to pray!*

What and how we pray definitely depend upon the content of our faith. There are many good books published on prayer as far as techniques go, but these often fail to guide the reader to the fullness of the life of prayer because they fail of Christian content. We can learn much from a Hindu swami, and certainly God can use many means, but we cannot in that way learn the nature and power of Christian prayer. There are also books on prayer that come from the pens of great pseudo-Christian spirits and thinkers which still, unfortunately, fall short of the Christian content of thought, and therefore also of faith. Great praying always roots in great believing, and believing has not only intensity but also doctrinal substance. Great praying swells up from the depths of great theology, a dynamic depth-understanding and acceptance of what God in Christ is and wills. Great praying springs out of depth-grasping and depth-appropriation of what God wills with us all and for us all. Great praying rises out of the vision and beauty of God himself, not isolated from the world, but in a yearning relation to save it, in a relation of sharp contrast in being and power. Hinduism says of man: Thou art that absolute, if thou wilt only recognize it. Buddhism says: Thou art not at all that absolute. The Christian faith says: Thou, absolute God, art that, and lo, I am the sinner that needs to be changed, and can be.

Prayer rises only as high as our doctrine of God. And our doctrine cannot be had apart from the steady devotion, which is to occasional devotions, as Saint Francis de Sales says, as a chimney to bellows. *Teach Us To Pray* is a significant book because it is rooted in a great doctrine of God. In prayer at its highest, God prays more than we, because we are caught up and compelled by the Holy Spirit. Not that we are not willing, not that our efforts are not needed, but rather that as God becomes real and more powerful in our lives, his infinite light, power, and love lay hold of our little lives beyond their usual capacity and make new creatures in Christ Jesus. The flood of his incomparable self simply sweeps along our little shallow eddies and pours itself forth upon the world with help and healing.

Then, too, right and powerful prayer must be keenly aware of the natural state of man. Too many treatises on prayer do not take account of the obvious fact that man is extremely frail and deeply stained with sin. The depth, steadiness, and stubbornness of sin are seldom the unmistakable background of modern books on prayer. We need to go to the root of man's despair and to the depths of man's guilt. Then, prayer ceases to be an offering to God of something with which he simply ought to be pleased. There is no merit in prayer in *God's* sight. Unless all self-sufficiency and self-satisfaction are crushed to bits, landing man in utter self-despair, he can never find the God-security which makes prayer pulse with heavenly power. For so it ought to pulse, when right. Some see man's sin in his natural state and never get beyond it. Naturally all have to live by grace through faith, always and ever. There can never be any merit or any boasting before God. In the light of God's Christ, the holy agape-love of which Professor Whiston speaks, all are declared sinners without a chance to fulfill the perfect law of God. Yet when forgiveness is real, there is also neither law nor trespass any longer. In that perspective or in that relation to God, faith grows more and more in all knowledge and we are increasingly perfected together. In that relation to God, tensions cease and we have "peace with God through our Lord Jesus Christ." In that state we are delivered "from this body of death" and cry "Abba, Father," since "there is now no condemnation for those who are in Christ Jesus," who live after the law of the Spirit which is joy and peace. So often in books on prayer either man's natural sinfulness is minimized or else the power of God to set man free and singing is throttled. *Teach Us To Pray* is significant in that its view of prayer roots in a Christian understanding of man, both before and after his conversion.

The temptations that come in our prayer life are

many and subtle. Those who have prayed consistently for years know that there seems to be no letup, that with new occasions or new stages, new and wiry temptations also set in. These temptations are obviously different, depending upon the kind of God we have and what is expected of prayer. What we need to go with the right theology of prayer is the right technique and the right instruction concretely to meet particular hindrances and temptations. Over the years I have found Professor Whiston's simple suggestions more and more important. They require constant cultivation. They are exceedingly simple to grasp with one's mind, but they require the long waiting for the harvest, which he writes about, for them to bear much fruit. My whole life has been enriched and changed by a few simple suggestions about prayer which I have heard Professor Whiston make in relation to prayer for enemies, prayer with the church offering, in the partaking of the Communion, in the way we wake and go to sleep, in the way we wait, even, for a red light to change. The new kind of consciousness, or the semi-autonomous consciousness of communion with God, comes slowly, but when it comes, all seems changed, and it really becomes hard even to imagine a life lived without almost uninterrupted fellowship with God. *Teach Us To Pray* not only roots in basic Christian faith, and in depth-understanding of both natural and redeemed man, but it has specific suggestions, both positively and with regard to our failures in prayer, and is, therefore, in our day invaluable equipment for the Christian life of prayer.

Then, too, Professor Whiston has for years directed schools of prayer and retreats. Numerous ministers and alert laymen are convinced that this is a central need of the churches. How can our cold, formal, half-dead churches ever get new life except it be breathed into them from above? How can the lump be changed unless there be at least potent leaven? For the crowd we need the cell. The old prayer meeting was once the thermometer of the church. Few churches can now run that kind of prayer meeting with genuine power. Yet we must nevertheless in some way cultivate adequately the devotional life. The suggestions of this book should be of great help to all traditions. The more activistic, evangelical groups will find the stress on silence and meditation hard to follow. They seemingly have to have something doing all the time. Yet why not try to find the steadier light and the deeper depth by these tried and true experiences of the saints of the ages? After all, Jesus went out all night to pray. He even withdrew from the important healing of the multitudes to find new power and rest in communion with his Father. One of the important helps of the book, to me, is the directions for effective group prayer and group devotion.

A recent inter-seminary conference at Yale had for its theme the preparation of the spiritual life, dividing the subject into motivation, cultivation, and application. As far as *Teach Us To Pray* is concerned, the first two topics are strongly dealt with, while the third is introduced, but not developed. Personal prayer for individuals in authority is important, by all means. We cannot slight this important aspect of Christian social action. But I have an idea that when we come to realize the relation between the Holy Spirit and the Church, on the one side, and the social and political problems, on the other, we shall come to see that there is both an indirect and a direct way of affecting the latter two in terms of the former two. The Christian fellowship through the Holy Spirit can reach and co-operate constructively with the responsible forces of the civic world. This can be done when in prayer, faith, and constructive action the Holy Spirit translates, transforms, and transmits the message and purpose of the Church for the whole world by means of the Spirit of God, the universal presence and operation by God in all. Much needs to be done on this topic, and I hope, therefore, that Professor Whiston will develop social prayer along some such line as I have suggested. It seems to me that neither quiet withdrawal, plus possibly individual prayer, nor mere direct social action can or will do the job that is needed. We need to combine prayer and intelligent action, the indirect and the direct approaches. It is to be hoped that some day his teaching will direct us further in the realm of the all-around application of the Christian prayer life to society. Yet he has shown even now the very heart of the matter which is almost invariably left out in treatments of social transformation. But something is yet to come for both sides of the need!

Best of all, this book is no mere theory. It rises out of the genuine prayer life of its author. The reader will feel himself caught by its power and purpose the more he is willing to let himself go with it. I have seldom been so genuinely convinced of the need of any single book as I am of this one. If it is read and used in the spirit in which it has been written, it will come as a fresh breeze of power to this desperately needy and despairing world. Every pastor who loves his people should read this book, and having been caught up in its spirit and having learned from its suggestions, he ought then to have his whole congregation, as far as possible, use this book together with him. For a sick world we need a praying church, that we may live, first of all right with God, in peace and power, but then also, in the second place, that our social and political dreads and insecurities may be done to death by the creative and redemptive power of Christian people.

NELS F. S. FERRÉ

Abbot Professor of Christian Theology,
The Andover Newton Theological School,
Newton Centre, Massachusetts

PART I

The Vision

And Jesus, when he came out, saw much people, and was moved with compassion toward them, because they were as sheep not having a shepherd: and he began to teach them many things.

MARK 6:34

And it came to pass, that, as he was praying in a certain place, when he ceased, one of his disciples said unto him, Lord, teach us to pray. . . .

And he said unto them, When ye pray, say, Our Father which art in heaven, Hallowed be thy name. Thy kingdom come. Thy will be done, as in heaven, so in earth.

Give us day by day our daily bread.

And forgive us our sins; for we also forgive every one that is indebted to us. And lead us not into temptation; but deliver us from evil.

LUKE 11:1-4

1

Teach Us to Pray

"LORD, TEACH US to pray." These words of one of the companions of Jesus, asked on behalf of himself and of his fellow-disciples, give also true expression to the deep yearning and hunger of people in every age since then. Who of us has not at some time had the thought that there must be far more to praying than we have yet known? Where can we find somebody who will tell us of the depths and breadths and riches of praying? But so often this is only a passing thought, and we do nothing about it. This book has its origin in the initiative of God, offering to men that for which they hunger and yearn, but know not how to find for themselves. This book is an invitation to all sorts and conditions of men to enter into the unique spiritual joy, love, peace, and power which come to us in praying.

Those for whom this request was made of Jesus were not men unaccustomed to the practice of praying. They were men who followed the Jewish practice of praying. But in their companionship with Jesus they had come to realize that in his praying there was depth, mystery, hidden meaning, richness beyond that which was in their own. They sensed, and sensed accurately, that part of the mysterious quality and power of Jesus' life lay in the intimate fellowship he had with his Father in, during, and through his praying. They too yearned to enter into that richer and deeper friendship with God, and turned to Jesus that he might be their guide and teacher.

Jesus' answer was to give them the prayer which we call the "Lord's Prayer." Certainly his intention was not simply that we should merely repeat these words as words, and then call our act "praying." Praying is something far more meaningful and significant than the mere recitation of particular words. Rather, in these words Jesus gave us the perfect standard for all our praying. In these simple words are enshrined the basic laws, principles, and standard of distinctively Christian praying.

Never can we exhaust the depth and significance of this one prayer. As we use this great prayer, given to us by the Master of praying, and enter into its depths and give ourselves up to its mighty power, there come to us insight and understanding far beyond all our expectation from so short and simply worded a prayer. As we use this one prayer more humbly and reverently, we find that it becomes truly the standard of all our praying.

This book is offered in all reverence as a guide and help for those — so many in number in every age — who never pray; for those who know not how to pray; for those who pray, but only intermittently and by "fits and starts"; for those who pray only in times of crisis, and then wish that they knew much more about true and deep praying; for all those who seek to pray, but find themselves inarticulate, lost, and bewildered in praying; for both clergy and laity who hunger and wistfully desire that somebody would come into their lives to teach them how to pray. The book is meant for those who think that they have no need of praying; for all those who are so busied with the work of the world and the social needs of men that they have no time or concern for God and see no relationship of praying to these human needs.

This book is also offered to those whose only knowledge of praying is limited to corporate worship in church on Sundays; to the many church officials, men and women, whose inner lives in the midst of church activities are often devoid of spiritual insight and resources; to the many hidden souls in every church and parish, who hunger and wait to be led into ever deeper ways of spiritual living; and to all those who seek within the Church for deeper, living friendship with God and with their fellow men.

This book is also offered to the many clergy, who in all their training for the ministry have never actually been taught "how to pray"; to the many clergy who after a few years in the active ministry come to realize their deep, spiritual inadequacy, and yearn secretly to be taught the sources and mysteries of spiritual fellowship with God, so that they may more truly and deeply be servants of God to their people.

Teach Us To Pray is not only intended for church people, laity and clergy; but also for the great number who are outside of the churches; those who are critical, prejudiced, or even hostile to the Church; those who find the churches a real stumbling block to God. May this book under God's mysterious providence fall into their hands and give them that which will meet patiently, understandingly, and humbly their honest discontent, and help them to interpret the deep hunger already existing in the depths of their being.

For the sceptic, the agnostic, the indifferent, the scoffer, and even for the atheist this book is meant; all of these are invited to read it through, and to practice as an experiment its very practical suggestions, leaving their minds open to the possibility that it contains much with which they will find themselves in hearty agreement, and some things which will express that which has for them been inarticulate. There may be more to praying than they have suspected.

This book also offers teaching for that great number of praying persons, whose use of prayer is only or predominantly self-petition. It is for them an invitation to explore and enter into those great expanses of praying which lie far beyond the confines of self-petition. All of us go through the stage of praying which is almost exclusively self-seeking. Then we are apt to arrive at a stage where we believe we are unselfish and concerned for others; but hidden deeply within us self-seeking and self-interest still operate. We are secretly seeking our own in our evident concern for others. We are willing to serve others because we profit thereby. This book seeks to lead such persons into distinctively Christian disinterestedness, where they will seek nothing for themselves, but only God's glory and blessing for their fellow men.

As we read and follow the teaching of this book we shall awaken to the realization that very much of our praying is not distinctively Christian. Much praying, even within Christian churches, varies little, if any, from that within religions that are non-Christian. Christian praying is distinctive, because in it man is set free from every trace of self-seeking by his utter devotion to the glory of God and his unselfish and loving concern for his fellow men. All sorts and conditions of men, in their hunger and thirst after deeper fellowship with God and with men, can do no better than to follow the disciples of old, and turn to Jesus Christ, and cry out, "Lord, teach us to pray."

There are probably no persons today who do not pray, at least sometimes, in their own special way. It may be that they pray only in times of crisis. But if we pray only in times of crisis, we all know that this kind of praying does not satisfy us. To pray in times of crisis, however, does remind us that we do not pray in times of fair weather, and may induce us to continue the practice of prayer when the immediate crisis is over. We have seen this happen in war years, and in the periods immediately following wars. During war many people engage in the practice of praying. Many churches introduce "war shrines" for prayer. With some people, wartime praying has led to the practice of praying; with others, once hostilities ceased, praying also stopped and many war shrines ceased to function. Crisis praying is apt to be simply petitional, and we instinctively sense how shallow our acquaintance is with God when our praying is no more than petition. We wonder and hunger how we may learn to penetrate into the depth and breadth, into the secrets and mysteries of praying that is distinctively Christian.

From time to time God sends into our lives a man or a woman of prayer, who stirs us profoundly. We sense that the notes of spiritual love, peace, joy, and power in their lives are rooted in their practice of praying. We feel something contagious both about their lives and about their praying which awakens in us a desire to learn from them about the secrets and mysteries of prayer. We wish that we too might know God and have, as they do, a living and intimate companionship with him. We start to pray; but when we seek to be our own teachers in prayer, we find ourselves at once confronted with many difficulties and perplexities, and with myriad distractions that annoy and defeat us. Temptations dishearten us, and we wish that somebody would teach us how to meet temptation victoriously. On many days we find our intention to pray broken by the busyness and pressure of the world upon our lives. We offer ourselves many excuses: it is hard to find time to pray; even when we make time, we know not what or how to pray; we start again to read the Bible but we find it a book very difficult to understand. Others, we know, get much satisfaction from their praying and from Bible reading; we so little. Though others find power, we find only discouragement. For us spiritual companionship is something about which we read but which we do not know how to experience.

Probably many persons either do not ever begin the practice of praying, or having begun it, soon abandon it, or pray only spasmodically and intermittently, because they have no satisfying or profound understanding of the purposes, principles, laws, and methods of prayer. The acts of prayer require first of all that we seek to understand them, before we begin to practice them. This book offers that understanding of praying upon which may be built a disciplined practice.

This book treats of the life of praying, and not simply of acts of prayer. Prayer has a life, as people have life. Prayer is born, grows, and may also die, unless it is persistently cared for and nourished. It is not merely the saying or the hearing of words labeled as prayers. True praying engages the whole person, utilizing all his powers and faculties. No other activity of man co-ordinates more fully all the powers of man's life than does praying. Moreover, no other activity can give unity and balance to man's life as can the life of praying.

The life of praying involves the willing acceptance and entering into the disciplines of training in prayer but they are means, not ends in themselves. Because we are weak in will, frail in goodness, and so apt to root religious practices in our emotions, we all need and can benefit greatly from wise training, accepted and entered into voluntarily. Especially in the beginning stages it can be of great help to us. Having undergone the disciplines of praying we shall reach that stage in which we shall joyfully and regularly desire to pray, and looking back over the years, we shall then give God thanks for all that we have learned in our praying, and we shall wonder how we previously ever got along without praying.

The life of distinctively Christian praying is difficult, but it is within the capacities of all men, regardless of their social or intellectual status. To say that the life of praying is difficult means only that it requires understanding, effort, patience, persistence, help; but God gives these freely to those who seek truly to enter into the life of prayer. This book offers understanding and practical suggestions about praying "to prepare the way of the Lord," and to turn us and to lead us to God himself, from whom this teaching has come. But much more than reading in a book about praying is required before one becomes a man of prayer. Once we have gained an understanding of the laws and principles of praying and have received practical suggestions in methods, then over and above this we must go to God himself, and let him lead us into the life of prayer.

Clergy and laity alike are in need of true and deep understanding of the laws, principles, and methods of Christian praying, and it will usually be found that they have the same common and basic needs. The very widespread assumption that Christians, by the very fact of their membership in the Christian Church, both know how to pray and do pray is one which will not stand much serious examination. The fact is that the Christian life of praying does not grow naturally and without nourishment. The physical body in its growth has not been entrusted to man's own conscious care. Rather it is under the control of what seem to be almost automatic processes. But it is not so with the life of praying. We do not naturally grow up into it. Unless we take pains and make an effort, it will not even be born, let alone grow. The life of praying is an infused life, given to us by God. To exhort men to pray is thus not enough, unless at the same time they are offered serious instruction as to how to pray, and led into actual praying.

Evidence is growing that, among both clergy and laity, men are eager and hungry to learn more fully and deeply of the life of praying. More and more men are coming to acknowledge frankly their abysmal ignorance concerning the all-important relationship with God in prayer. Men instinctively look to the Church and to the clergy for help and for teaching in prayer. Where else may men look? Men may be shy at giving voice to this deep, inner need and hunger; but they know their need, and when such help in praying is offered to them, many eagerly respond.

When we reflect upon it, the ignorance of all of us concerning the life of praying is in no way an amazing fact. For when we examine the curricula and material commonly used in Sunday schools, we search almost in vain for any sustained, serious, and systematic attempt to teach and train children, parents, or teachers how to pray. At the time when youth enters into full and responsible membership in the Church, although they are exhorted to pray, yet seldom are they instructed as to the laws, principles, and methods of praying.

Only in a very small number of churches or communities have schools of prayer been held. Everywhere it is taken for granted that Christians do pray, and know how to pray. The result is that with the exception of petition and less occasional thanksgiving, the riches and depths of the life of Christian praying are commonly unknown.

When we turn to the clergy themselves, we are equally at a loss to understand the foundation for the common assumption that the clergy, simply by the fact of their calling, are therefore men of prayer. The clergy themselves know (and many of them are frank to admit it) the falsity of this assumption. In the theological seminaries of most of the churches one must search long and far to find courses offering serious and systematic instruction in the spiritual life. Here again it is taken for granted that the theological student has somehow already acquired the knowledge, understanding, discipline, and practice of truly Christian praying.

Theological education has been and still is predominantly intellectual — the imparting of correct conceptions about God. The divinity schools are theological and intellectual in emphasis, rather than spiritual. Too little attention has been given to the all-important task of training, educating, and disciplining the interior, spiritual life of the seminary student. In actual practice it is commonly limited to daily chapel services, to occasional quiet days, or to even less occasional retreats. Much more than this must be done to assure that the theological student becomes truly a man of prayer.

The boards of examining chaplains can witness to the common lack of any established practice of intelligent and disciplined praying among the young men about to begin their active ministries. When bishops and superintendents make their periodical visitations, how very seldom is it that they examine the clergyman as to his spiritual life and discipline. Almost every other matter than the spiritual life is dealt with, but the most central matter of all is simply taken for granted.

The life of the minister is not one in which it is easy to be a man of prayer. The pattern of church life often makes it well-nigh impossible for the minister to dwell in or even enter upon praying. Very seldom is real and adequate provision made for him to secure that necessary solitude, without which the life of praying is almost impossible. Myriad demands are made upon his time and energies. He is expected to be an able preacher; to conduct services; to be a wise and efficient and successful money raiser and administrator; to take an active and leading part in all important civic functions and organizations; to be familiar with all recent books and movements. In short, it is demanded that he be a man of the world; too infrequently is it demanded that he be a man of God, a man of prayer.

Ministers in all of the churches are increasingly coming to acknowledge their lack of deep and abiding spiritual foundations and resources for their most difficult work. Loneliness pervades the lives of many clergymen. They are not apt to speak to others of this deep loneliness, nor do they always use the word "loneliness," even though the feeling is present. They say that they are "exhausted" or "under too much strain"; and their friends and physicians, knowing nothing of this spiritual loneliness, say in all sincerity and truthfulness that they have a "nervous breakdown."

There exists then dire need in clergy and in laity alike for serious and wise understanding and disciplined practice of the life of truly Christian praying. Basic and fundamental teaching and training in the Christian life of praying should be the normal expectation of every Christian. The laws and principles of the life of praying should be even more familiar to him than are the laws of the natural sciences. Methods of praying should be made familiar to every Christian, whatever his status and condition in life. The life of distinctively Christian praying is not intended for the few and for the elite, but for all men.

The teaching and the suggested disciplines contained in this book are those which have been widely used by the author over many years now, in different sections of this land. They have been given in many schools of prayer, both denominational and interdenominational; as teaching in the spiritual life given in many retreats for both clergy and laity; as instruction given to theological students in the Church Divinity School of the Pacific, as an integral and central part of their training for the Christian ministry; as material presented in sermons in parishes and missions, seeking to teach and to guide parish people in living the life of the spirit; and in the work of spiritual direction with many individuals, both men and women, of greatly varying ages and backgrounds.

Thus the teaching contained in this book is not simply theoretic, but has been tested over many years in the most exacting of all fields — that of human lives active in the world.

* * * *

God sees and knows fully and perfectly every need of man, and in compassion for him ever takes the initiative to meet his true needs. This book has had its birth and growth from the initiative of God, and is now presented in the hope that, in God's providence, it may reach individual men and satisfy and meet their deepest need — their need for him.

Lord: Teach us to pray;
Make us to pray.

PART II

"Founded Upon a Rock"

If anyone comes to me and listens to this teaching of mine and acts upon it, I will show you whom he is like. He is like a man who was building a house, who dug deep and laid his foundation upon the rock, and when there was a flood the torrent burst upon that house and could not shake it, because it was well built. But the man who listens to it, and does not act upon it, is like a man who built a house on the ground without any foundation. The torrent burst upon it, and it collapsed at once, and the wreck of that house was complete.

LUKE 6:47-49

From *The Bible, An American Translation*, by Smith and Goodspeed. Used by permission of the University of Chicago Press.

2

The Initiative of God

WHERE DOES THE action of prayer begin? Often, both in our praying and in our worshiping, we tend to think of ourselves as the starting point. We seek God; and we hope that God will respond to our seeking. This perspective in surveying our praying is very natural to our self-centeredness. We can learn much about God and much about ourselves from this common point of view. This book, however, is written from a very different perspective — that it is not man, but God, who takes the initiative in the action and life of praying. We shall learn that we can see more accurately, more deeply, and more fully from this vantage point than from any other.

In praying, as in every religious action, the first and central agent is never man, but always God. Long before we begin to pray at all, God has already been acting in and upon us, preparing the way for our response. This is God's "prevenience." True, much of this prevenient action of God is at first hidden from us. God operates without our consciousness or our help. The theologians call this prior action of God "the prevenience of God." Once we become awakened to its truth and significance, we find that this prevenience alone can account adequately for our part in the action of praying.

We do not often hear this great Christian doctrine of prevenience taught or proclaimed by the clergy. Probably many of the laity have never even heard of such a doctrine. Yet, in the life of Christian praying, an understanding and acceptance of the conviction of prevenience is an absolute essential to any true and deep comprehension of the relation between God and man. Belief in God's prevenience will throw much needed light upon the specific role which man plays in the life of prayer. This book is written from the deep and truly Christian viewpoint that praying is first and foremost that which God does for us, and to us, and in us. Only after we grasp this can we then begin to understand the work which we must do in praying.

God does not wait until we first seek after him before he acts toward us redemptively. We ignore him, forget him, rebel against him. Yet he is always active in seeking to lead us into that saving friendship with himself, that friendship of which even the highest human friendship is only a most inadequate token. No human friendship is even to be compared with the friendship which God seeks to bestow upon us. The friendship he gives is unique.

When we begin to awaken to God and respond to his prevenient action in and upon us, even though we may be unaware of it, very much has already happened to us. We take our conscious part in the life of praying only late in the whole process. But behind our first response to God lies the long, prior, preparatory work of God. As we come to study the purposes of God in the various kinds of prayer, we shall realize this more and more. All of our actions in praying are always responses to God's prior action.

Care in the use of words is much needed here. Thus the common religious expression "love of God" can so often mean to self-centered man his own love toward God, rather than the much more stupendous conception of God's amazing love toward man. For as we grow in the life of Christian devotion, we find ourselves waking more and more to the amazingness of God's love for us, the sinful. We may start our religious life with the belief that we are worthy of God's love; but when we learn truly to pray and as we gain from God deeper insight into our unworthiness and sinfulness, we can no longer claim God's love, or take it for granted. His love for us becomes the most amazing fact of the whole religious life. Then we shall be ready for the great words of St. John: "We love him, because he first loved us." For the heart of the Christian gospel is not at all that man loves God, but that God loves man, the sinner.

To enter upon intimate friendship with God in praying would truly be presumptuous and hopeless, if we depended upon our own feeble and partial wisdom, our own weak and intermittent energies, and only on our own frail goodness. How can the little creature, man, blinded as he is by sin and imprisoned in self-centeredness, ever hope to attain Heaven and have fellowship with God? But Christian praying is founded upon the mighty wisdom, love, and goodness of God, and upon his prevenience. Therefore we can rejoice in full confidence and hope and trust, and gladly submit our lives to his action in the life of prayer. Christian praying will be to us the staggering proclamation of God's search for man, freely to give man fellowship with himself, and not of man's blind and futile search for God. We must look for the initiative and main action in praying not in ourselves, but in God.

Our conception of praying will alter greatly, and for good, as the doctrine of the divine prevenience becomes for us a living conviction. It will save our praying from being presumptuous, and our lives from the deadly sin of pride, which inevitably insulates our lives from God. Always we are to interpret our desire and impulse to pray as having its adequate explanation only in the prior, hidden action of God in and upon our lives, drawing us and pulling us to him. Realizing this, we shall be compelled to give more serious attention to every dim, faint stirring within us, and to respond at once in holy obedience to that inner voice. We learn ever more deeply of our terrible power to misuse and neglect the grace given us of God, but also of the wondrous new life and new selfhood which issue from every acceptance of his gifts and from obedience to his will.

In the relationship between God and man it is always God who is on the scene first, who acts first, who takes the initiative, — and all of this long before we begin our part in the action. Praying, on our part, is our response to God's prevenience.

Creator and Creature

Who is this One to whom we pray? Who are we who pray? What is God; and what is man? The answers to these questions are most important, for our moods and our methods of praying are largely determined by our answers to these questions about the relationships between God and man during praying.

Widespread and common is the belief that man is made in the "image of God." By this is usually meant that there is in man an inner core which is by nature akin to God. When we consider the biblical usage of this term "image of God" the facts are most interesting and revealing, and they in no way support the popular belief concerning man. In the Old Testament the word is used for man as intended by God in creation. Its use is limited to the early chapters of the Book of Genesis. In the New Testament it is never used as a description of man as he now is. Jesus, and not man, is called "the image of God." Man's claim that he already is in part divine rather than that he is to become, by the action of God, remade into the likeness of Jesus Christ, is in fact a sign of man's radical conceit and pride — which is sin. The origin of the term "image of God" lies rather in Hellenistic than in Hebraic-Christian sources. The Greeks thought of man as being by nature divine, so far as his soul was concerned. In a later chapter we shall face the conflict between the Hellenistic and Christian conceptions of man as expressed in the terms "resurrection" and "immortality."

The biblical conviction of important distinctions between God and man, kept steadfastly in our minds, sharpens our conceptions of the Christian life of praying. Our hope in religion lies in the fact that God in most important ways is not as we are; not simply in degree, but distinctively and qualitatively, God is different from us. In no respect is this fundamental unlikeness more sharply and decisively brought out than in the distinction expressed by the words "Creator" and "creature." This great Jewish-Christian conviction enshrined in the doctrine of creation safeguards a most important truth concerning the basic inequality existing in the relationship between God and man in praying.

To call God the "Creator" is to assert a basic difference between God and man. Whereas God has his existence in himself, utterly independent of every other being, man has not his existence in himself, apart from all else. Man as creature is utterly dependent upon God, both directly and indirectly, for his origin and preservation at each moment of his life. Thus the relation of God to man is very different from that of man to God. God does not require us for his own existence. Even though the whole of creation should cease to exist, God would still be God.

This basic distinction is also expressed in the difference between "Isness" and "Becoming," terms so often used in the teaching of Baron von Hügel. God is; man is becoming. God does not change or grow or become God. He is God. Man is in the midst of a process of becoming something he has never been before. Man is unfinished, incomplete, growing, changing. The ancient liturgical refrain has much still to teach our humanistic age, with its great and deep cry:

> Glory be to thee, O Father,
> And to thee, O Son,
> And to thee, O Holy Ghost:
>
> For as thou wert in the beginning,
> Thou art now,
> And ever shalt be;
> World without end. Amen.

A study of Christian theology based not simply upon intellectual reasoning, but also upon the data of Christian worship and devotion, will give us the deepest and truest insights into essential Christian beliefs.

As Creator, God is both the origin and source of continuance of everything that has existence. It is not simply that God causes things to come into existence and that they then maintain themselves. Rather it is that creatures continue in existence only in so far and for so long a time as God directly wills. Without his continuing creative and preserving action at each moment, they would fall back at once into that nothingness from which he called them in creation.

We are faced here with an utterly insoluble and even inconceivable mystery. Thus when we speak of God as the Creator of the universe, we do not mean that he took already existing matter, or even matter in a state of chaos, and then upon it simply superimposed order. On the contrary, we mean that nothing but God existed at all, and that by a sheer act of God's will there was brought into being both the order and the material.

All things were made by him; and without him was not any thing made that was made.   JOHN 1:3

Such a conception truly staggers all our human conceiving, since such an act forever lies outside all our human experience. Man can only take already existing material and then alter and rearrange it. To acknowledge this great mystery of creation will ever keep us humble in the life of praying, keeping us mindful of the incalculable and utterly unpayable debt which we owe to the creating and preserving God. We begin our part in the life of praying already in the status of debtors.

When we reflect humbly and prayerfully upon our own physical existence, we needs must acknowledge that the larger part of the functioning and control of our bodies and minds has not been entrusted to our own conscious control. The action of our lungs, the beating of our heart, the functioning of our nervous system, the digestive and the recuperative work of the body — none of these is entirely under our own direction. They function for us and not by us. To describe their operation merely in physiological terms, or as being the work of "abstract laws," does not explain them at all adequately or meaningfully. We must cease shrinking from the bold biblical conviction and faith that it is God himself who governs and operates these processes for us. The Psalmist saw to the heart of the matter in his cry:

It is he that hath made us, and not we ourselves.

Thus we shall think of God as repairing and refreshing our wearied bodies and minds in sleep; and of him as waking us to conscious life each morning. This conviction of devotion is enshrined in the very ancient Morning Collect:

. . . God, who hast safely brought us to the beginning of this day . . .

as also in the modern prayer:

And since it is of thy mercy, O gracious Father, that another day is added to our lives . . .

Man is creature. That is the appointed status of man, a status from which he can never escape, either in this earthly life or in that life which lies beyond the grave. At every moment of his existence, both here and there, created man is utterly dependent upon his Creator. God works imperceptibly but powerfully through all the myriad channels we call primary and secondary, immediate and final. We err greatly when we speak of God as being simply one cause among many. God is never simply a secondary cause. Working in and through all other causes, he is The Cause.

Man has been made by God, for God's purpose. Man has not been made for himself. We are made for God, for his glory, and for intimate fellowship with him. This is the central purpose of our being here, and once we have awakened to it and accepted it, the whole of our life upon earth takes on a new and satisfying significance. But because many have never heard of this purpose, never been taught what is the central purpose of life, they often wonder for what end they are here on earth; and they never know the radiant, joyful life which comes to those who live for God, by God, and in God.

Man's very existence, both in its beginning and in its continuance, is the gift of God. God has intended that man, his creature, shall live joyfully acknowledging this basic and inescapable dependence upon his Maker. Man should look out and up to his Creator, the very source of his being; and thus be truly God-centered, with every part of his life related to God. Out of this sense of dependence would then issue thankfulness, that mood which deeply characterized the lives of the earliest Christians. The Christian has an ever deepening, ever growing realization of the immensity and the wonder of his relation to God, and of the incalculable and unpayable debt which he owes to his Creator. In turn, thankfulness will issue in glad obedience, an obedience so different from that imposed from without that Christians call it "holy obedience."

Very different from this is man's actual status — self-centeredness. Man is fallen. We are not that which God intended us to be. We are not even that which we know we ought to be. The biblical doctrine of the Fall, expressed in the form of the ancient myth of Adam and Eve, does proclaim a terrible and undeniable truth concerning ourselves — any self-willed existence is sinful.

The heart of the matter is that we have refused to live under the terms set by our Creator — in God-centeredness, dependence, thankfulness, and holy obedience, by which alone we can become truly sons of God. Man has seized himself and turned his back upon his Creator. Man has become self-willed and self-centered, seeking to make himself the center and goal of his own existence. He has dared to believe that the body and life, entrusted to him by God in order that he might become a son of God, are his own to be used as he pleases and for his own pleasure and will.

For the wise, loving, powerful, patient providence and sovereignty of God, man has presumed to substitute blind self-rule, based upon his own partial and distorted knowledge, his own frail goodness, his own selfish will. Thus has man turned God's good earth into his own hell. Man has become imprisoned in himself and in the world. A powerful "kingdom of man" has grown up, with man seeking to do those works for which only God is adequate. Man seeks to believe that he is God. So deeply has man fallen into self-centeredness that even after many disastrous centuries he still stubbornly persists in believing that he can and will save himself and create a world to his own liking. Refusing to accept as gifts the myriad blessings of God, refusing to live upon the divine charity, man has instead sought to seize and to hold the earth and all that it contains. But God has answered man by sending fear into his heart: fear of his fellow men, fear of the uncertain future, and fear of death, when man will be stripped of all of his possessions and must be alone with himself and God.

With man's rebellion against God and his attempt to exercise sovereignty over his own life, he has ceased to be thankful to God. He has so blinded himself that he does not know that the origin of these many good things is God. He believes that he can earn them and win them by competition and strife. Then he fears lest they be taken away from him. His spirit of disobedience to God has so infected his whole nature that now he cannot even obey himself or the codes and laws which he has made. Man lives as if there were no God. He is blind to the presence of God, and deaf to his voice. Man is lost.

The praying of one who believes and knows that

he is lost, and will remain lost until God finds him, will be a very different kind of praying from that of one who holds the conviction that he can and will save himself. The life of Christian praying will greatly deepen in us the sense of our deep-seated, sinful selfhood, and of the inadequacy of ourselves to be born into and grow up in the new selfhood of the spirit. But always this deepening sense of sin is accompanied by the much greater willingness to depend upon God's grace. Self-despair, if it remains despair, is tragedy. But where self-despair leads us to trust in God's grace and adequacy, it brings courage and enablement and peace, and becomes an experience for which we give God thanks.

In true and earnest praying we turn as creature to our Creator, ever mindful of our rightful status of dependence, joyfully and willingly giving to him our thankful obedience, placing him always in the central place. Christian praying is always that of creature praying to his Creator, God. Upon this foundation is built the house of prayer.

3

Immortality or Eternal Life by Resurrection?

THE RELATIONSHIP OF the doctrines of Resurrection and Immortality to praying, at first sight, may not be apparent, but in these doctrines are set forth vividly and clearly two conceptions of man, — one Christian, the other non-Christian. Until we waken to, understand, and accept the abiding and irreconcilable contrast between immortality, as that selfhood centered and organized about itself, and resurrection, as the new selfhood centered and organized about God, how can we know what man's life of praying should be?

In no respect is fallen man's presumption more clearly to be perceived than in the conception of his own natural immortality. Conviction of immortality of the soul of man, widely held among Christians, is not a doctrine of the Bible. The New Testament firmly proclaims that God "only hath immortality," and this implies that man is by nature mortal. In the great historic creeds of Christianity nothing is said about the immortality of the soul of man, but instead it is forcefully and clearly asserted that our hope for everlasting life — or as John prefers to call it, "Eternal Life" — is rooted and grounded in God's mighty act of resurrection. We do not believe that we continue our existence on our own volition. We believe that God himself will raise us from death into new life and new selfhood, which eventually will be fully and completely God-centered.

To the Hellenic mind the Christian doctrine of resurrection was an affront; it seriously belittled the dignity of man. For the Greek, man was a pure spirit living temporarily and unnaturally in a body as its prison-house. Man as spirit or soul was immortal by nature. Salvation consisted in being freed from the hampering confines of a body, and living as a pure and disembodied spirit in the heavenly world. It was only the body which died in death. For the Greek the soul did not die, for it could not perish. The soul, organized about itself, continued to exist independently of God. Its immortality was in no essential way dependent on or related to God.

To thinking Christians this Hellenic conception of man seemed the rankest blasphemy and presumption. Their belief in God as Creator and man as creature was a very different conception of man. Death was for man the total stop and end, not only of his body but also of his spirit. The whole man, conceived in terms of a unity, died. It was therefore required that God should, by a mighty and mysterious act of resurrection, raise not simply a part, but the whole of man. What is raised in resurrection is not simply a body or a mind or a soul, but the whole self. Just as in our entrance into earthly life God bestowed upon us a body with many faculties and possibilities of development, so in resurrection God the Creator bestows upon us a new and heavenly body, a body utterly beyond our present earthly powers of comprehension, to be the vehicle of the new eternal life. Resurrection is the second creation of man by God. Man must learn unmistakably from the experience of death that his risen existence depends not upon himself, but upon God.

Thus because of the experience of death, man would face God's judgment upon his earthly life and awaken to his true state, as seen by God. Just as every instant of his earthly existence from birth to death depended utterly upon God as creator and preserver, so too the beginning and continuance of life after death is also utterly dependent upon God. Man does not have life in or by or for himself. His life is from God, for God, and by God; so, too, by God, for God, and from God is his death.

God's raising of us from death — resurrection — holds a central and key position in the Christian life. Resurrection is entrance into full eternal life.

To be aware of this will have consequences upon the mood and quality of our relationships with God in praying. Belief that our soul is immortal by nature, apart from God's will, will lead us subtly into feelings of self-sufficiency and self-centeredness, insulated from and independent of God. When we are convinced by and committed to belief in resurrection, we find deepened and strengthened in us the note of utter dependence upon God, issuing in undying thankfulness. It will keep ever before us the note of inescapable divine judgment of our lives. It will impel us even within this earthly life to expect and accept and obey the myriad divine judgments upon our lives.

We are not simply seeking to get "back home" to a life which we originally had; but to enter into a new life and a new selfhood, which we have never before known or guessed, and which is a mystery to us. We are — to use biblical imagery — "strangers and pilgrims" going into a land and a life where we have never before been. In the life of praying, we therefore seek and welcome divine guidance and remaking through renunciation of the old self-centered existence and being born into that new selfhood which is centered in God.

Our goal is not simply the mere continuance of this distinctively human kind of existence, but through resurrection entrance and growth into eternal life with God. Our goal as Christians is to pass over from self-centered life into God-centered life. It begins here in this earthly life; it is fulfilled and perfected in the life beyond death.

Redeemer and Redeemed

Only God knows what man should be, what man actually is, and what man may become. He alone knows truly and fully all that must happen to man, if he is to attain to that eternal life to which God is calling him, and which alone can transform and glorify with a new radiance and spiritual joy all of man's earthly life. We, even at our best, can only dimly and partially know ourselves as we now are, or what we may become. For God's intention is that we are to put on that new selfhood, which has as its center not self but God, and which we have never before known. We are born, and we grow into that new selfhood only through a long process of progressive mortification of the old self-centered existence. This venture into the new life of the spirit, involving the full renunciation of the present life as it is lived unrelated to God, requires faith and courage.

All of our own knowledge of ourselves and of the world is grossly distorted by our own selfishness. The self-centered man cannot find God anywhere — in people or in things. He cannot hope, as long as he remains selfish, to understand the

God-centered life. The God-minded man, however, can and does understand the self-minded man. The divine wisdom is given only to those who are awakened to the nothingness of all purely human knowledge. For all real truth comes from God; apart from him man cannot know the truth that saves.

God's concern for man is something far deeper and greater than to save him from his misery, hardship, and folly. Man must be saved from himself as sinful. But this requires that the old self-made man, fashioned in self-centeredness, must die; and that the new man in Jesus Christ be born and grow. "Ye must be born again" of the Spirit. For this double work of renunciation and of rebirth only God is adequate in knowledge, in love, in power, in patience. Man cannot do this for himself. It must be done for him by God.

All self-chosen renunciations are futile and miss the central issue, and thereby perpetuate self-centeredness. The goal of this interior warfare is that the self — made in selfishness — shall die. This work of bringing about the death of the self-centered man is God's work, not ours. But man will not let God do this work in and upon him until he is awakened fully and decisively to his own radical sinfulness and is prepared to go through that lowly doorway of self-despair. It is only when man cries out, not only with his lips, but from his heart, "Alone, I cannot," that he can hear that still, small voice of the Indwelling Spirit speaking the saving word, "No, you cannot; but I can. Come unto me." Self-despair passes over into trust in God. Man finds that a new life and a new power enter into his life, giving him rebirth into a new selfhood of the spirit that brings him peace, power, and joy.

God's Christ is the redemptive pattern and power by which man's salvation is to be accomplished. In the Christ of God the power and paralysis of sin has been decisively broken. In him we have held up before us clearly and triumphantly God's man; and we are bidden to fasten our eyes upon him. Here is the one life in which the Father's name has been perfectly hallowed; the Father's kingdom come; the Father's will done. Here is the one life which, because of his intimate fellowship with the Father, has been victorious, spiritually joyful, free. But redemption does not mean simply that this life is held up before us to behold. If we are left to ourselves, imprisoned in the power and kingdom of sin, and simply enjoined by the use of our own energies to make ourselves repentant and righteous — *that* is nothing short of utter tragedy and despair. For to become like Christ is what none of us can ever accomplish by ourselves. To accomplish that, no amount of time or encouragement could ever suffice; we need **Christ**.

God's redemption of man through his Christ

is much more than holding before us a pattern of perfect holiness. We perish not from lack of a pattern, nor from insufficient knowledge. We know that already there is a wide gulf between what we ought to do and that which we do: in that gulf is sin. What we perish from is sin. If we are to be saved from self-centeredness, it must be by the coming into our lives of another kind of life — God's kind of life; and salvation must be his work in and upon us. That is what God does for us, to us, and in us by his Christ. The Christ of God comes to us and engrafts his own victorious and holy life into our life — as yeast in dough; and so we become new selves in Christ.

But man offers mighty resistances to God's redemptive action, both before and after his acknowledgment of his sinning. God's Christ searches for us and finds us. Finding us, he judges us and lovingly convicts us of sin. When we acknowledge and confess his judgment of us to be true, then he saves us. But man in his deep and subtle pride does not easily confess his sinfulness. Man is willing sometimes to acknowledge that he needs help. He seeks to believe that what he needs is help only against his environment and circumstances.

But God's Christ compels us finally to learn that what we must be saved from is not God's world, but from our self-centered selfhood. Therefore only the very humble and meek can accept God's gift of salvation in Christ Jesus. We prefer to call our trouble misfortune or mistake. We dislike the basic religious word "sin." In fact, that word has almost ceased to exist in our ordinary vocabulary. We prefer to call sin by some prettier, more up-to-date name — neurosis, delinquency, incompatibility. But God's name for sin is sin.

Slowly over the long years of our life God's Christ pursues us, bringing to naught all of our quasi-attempts to save ourselves without his help, and to make atonement from our side with God. At last we turn and face God's Christ, and know beyond all doubting that alone we cannot save ourselves, and certainly not anybody else. Only Christ can save. Man is sinner. Jesus is Redeemer.

4

The Indwelling Spirit

GOD WORKS IN man both from outside as Transcendent, in his work of providence; and also from within, in the work which he does as the Indwelling Spirit. The main work of the life of praying will always be that of the Indwelling Spirit.

The Indwelling Spirit is the gift from the Father and the Son to man. Simply from the fact of his physical birth, man is not thereby a child of God. Physical birth into human existence only gives man the status of creaturehood over against the Creator, God — the status of sinning creaturehood. But from the very beginning of the infant baby's life God is redemptively concerned. He wills to bestow upon the child a second birth, birth of the spirit, which is to be the beginning of a new status and relationship with himself — that of sonship by adoption and grace.

The significance of the Indwelling Spirit is not something which we readily or easily accept. But God's indwelling of us is a vital prerequisite for

THE INDWELLING SPIRIT 45

the full living of the life of distinctively Christian praying.

Men prefer to think of their lives as having by nature an element of divinity in them. "Are we not by nature an immortal soul?" They acknowledge that their physical bodies as such are subject at last to physical death. But they believe that a part of their nature, the soul, is not subject at all to death. This conception is enshrined in their conception of the natural immortality of the soul.

But the New Testament picture of man is that he is a unity of being, and that it is the whole man, and not simply a part of him, that is to be saved by God. Man needs to be saved not simply from his body, as though, when set free from that, all will be well with him. We know that mind and spirit and will, as well as body, are infected with sin. The whole man — body, mind, spirit, will — must learn to die to its old self-centered existence, and be reborn into the new life and new selfhood of the spirit. The Christian doctrine of the Indwelling Spirit stands unequivocally for this double need of man — the renunciation of the life lived under the reign of sin, and the rising up into newness of life and the putting on of the new life in Jesus Christ.

From the moment that a baby is born into existence, great powers of evil beat upon its life, seeking to enthrall it and own it. There is its own inherited sinfulness, the evil still powerful in the lives of the family members, and the ever active powers of evil operative in society. But God comes and dwells within that little life, ever pressing upon it not only from without, but also from within. The Indwelling God seeks to guide and inspire it, mold and shape it into the form of that new life which the New Testament calls eternal life. It is right here that the great warfare of the spirit begins, long before we waken to it and take any conscious part in it. For the indwelling of God in us marks the beginning of a lifelong process of remaking, of passing from life lived by self into that new life which lives for and by God.

Both parents and Church are to look upon each individual life as being the direct, immediate, personal concern of God, and to hold as the true goal of this life that it should become truly a child of God and an inheritor of eternal life. The Church must never cease proclaiming to all men that this eternal life is not man's by nature. It can be man's only by an act of adoption on God's part, followed by the hard work on man's part of self-renunciation and remaking in co-operation with God's grace. Without God's decisive act of adoption to begin this work, and his continuing grace, all is in vain.

The Indwelling God knows us from within, as we cannot possibly know ourselves. He knows that

THE INDWELLING SPIRIT 47

we were made for him, for his glory, and for intimate fellowship with him, that so we may live here on earth in the vision, power, peace, and joy of eternal life. Unto the Indwelling Spirit our hearts are wholly open, our every desire known; from him we can hide no secrets. We know only a small part of our total being, that part which we call the conscious mind. But the Indwelling Spirit knows us through and through. He knows all that we are and thus all that we need. He is ever working to inspire and guide us. He pleads with us, rebukes us, commands us, woos us.

We know from long experience that we have the terrible power to ignore God and to grieve him by our disobedience and willfullness, our blindness and deafness. But wherever we go, and whatever we do, the Indwelling Spirit is ever within us and active in us. Never will he abandon us. The versicle used in the Book of Common Prayer is well deserving of our notice; in it we cry out from our hearts, "Take not Thy Holy Spirit from us." We know that we well deserve to have the Indwelling Spirit utterly forsake and abandon us. We are not worthy at all that he should dwell in us. But we also know that should he abandon us, we should be utterly lost forever. Therefore we cry out that deep and urgent cry, "Take not Thy Holy Spirit from us."

In the life of praying it will always be a pre-

condition that we have "received the Spirit" —
e.g. that we have awakened to the fact of the Indwelling Spirit in our lives, to which we have heretofore been blind; and that we want him and entreat him to act in us even against our own will. Without the Indwelling Spirit, we can do nothing. Within our lives, if we are willing and obedient, there goes on unceasingly the great work of God accomplishing in us the work of praying. Except the Indwelling Spirit lay the foundation of praying, we build in vain the house of prayer.

God – Untempted and Sinless

The distinction between God as the untempted and as the sinless, and man as the tempted and the sinful is a very important one, and vital, if we are to become victors in this inner warfare between the self-centered and the God-centered selfhoods. The life of Christian praying has as one of its main purposes the interpretation to man of his temptations and sins, and the giving to him of the spiritual wisdom and power to be victorious over them. In our temptations and in our sinnings we turn for help and power to God, who is not tempted and who cannot sin.

God is the Holy One. In God there is no evil at all. There is nothing in his life to which evil can make any appeal. God is always totally and resolutely set against every form of evil. By nature he cannot be tempted, and therefore he cannot sin. We rejoice that there is One who is both untempted and sinless.

But with man the case is very different. Man's life is ever subject to temptation and therefore to the danger of sinning. There is something in man's nature to which evil can and does make a strong appeal. Just as the evil outside us makes its appeal to an evil that lies within us, so too the God outside us makes his appeal to something dwelling in us — the Indwelling Spirit which is God. And just as something within us leaps out to invite in the external evil, which is ever ready to invade our lives, so too something within us — the Indwelling Spirit — leaps out on our behalf to invite in the full and mighty action of the transcendent, redemptive God. Man is radically unlike God. St. Augustine has carefully expressed this basic difference between our life and God's by asserting that whereas God cannot sin, man at best is only able not to sin.

To some this seems at first sight to place God so far from any understanding or sympathy with our human experiences of temptation and sinning that we should be utterly unable to find any help from him. We are inclined to believe that it is only the tempted that can understand temptation, and the sinful the experience of sinning. It is true here that Paul is closer to us than Christ in sharing our common experiences. But we need to heed carefully the warning of Baron von Hügel that Christ, and not Paul, is to be in these matters our guide and our surest help. Just because Paul had been Paul the deep sinner, he could never therefore be the Paul which might have been possible had he not the history and eternal consequences of past sinning. So, too, St. Augustine would have been more truly Christian and more truly our guide today had he not first been the radical sinner of his pre-Christian days. We must never forget that there are eternal consequences to all sinning, and an eternal loss.

For light here we must look to Jesus. He, and not his Jewish contemporaries, saw most deeply and keenly and truly into the sins and the needs of the Jewish people. They who had sinned could not see their own sinfulness, for sin always involves blindness. Our yielding to temptation, and our falling into sin, utterly and permanently disqualify us from realizing fully our own sins or those of others. The only one who could see and redeem the sins of the Jews was the One utterly free from sin.

In our temptations and in our sinnings we turn then to One who can never sin, to One whom evil can never deceive nor make to accept any compromise; to One who is ever steadfastly set against all evil. His righteousness stands fast and abides forever, never failing. He alone can see our

THE INDWELLING SPIRIT

temptations and know our sin with the clear eyes of holy love. He knows, as we cannot, the irrationality and stupidity and seriousness of our sinning.

God is the Holy One. Yet there is an all-important distinction between the belief in the holiness of God in the Old Testament and that which is contained in the New. God is the Holy One. Therefore, claims the Old Testament, God will have no contact with sinful man. Only when man ceases to be sinful and makes himself righteous will the Holy God open to man his friendship. In the Old Testament, until man repents, God removes himself to a vast distance from man, holding himself aloof and distant. This post-Exilic emphasis in Judaism on holiness led in practice to the belief in a distant, aloof, remote, and utterly transcendent God.

But in Jesus' life and teaching we have given to us a new and amazing correction of this ancient conviction. True, the Old Testament conviction of the steadfast opposition and hostility of God to all sinfulness is the background upon which the New Testament teaching takes its stupendous meaning. God is the Holy One. Not for one moment does Christ minimize or alter the seriousness and depth of sin and of God's hostility to it. But the conclusion he draws from this premise is an amazing one. Therefore, says Christ, God presses his holy life close to that of sinful man, in order that his holiness may burn up in man every trace of sin. In Jesus we see that the divine holiness is always redemptive and ever takes the initiative. The holiness of God is not and cannot be contaminated by the sins of men. Left to himself in his state of sin, man could never even hope to attain friendship with God.

Christian praying gives us as nothing else can give this deepened sense of the awful holiness of God, and by contrast also the deepened sense of our own radical and deep-seated sinfulness. In Christian praying we waken to our desperate need for divine redemption. God teaches us more and more of our need of surrendering our lives to his redeeming action in and upon us. These convictions give urgency and seriousness to our life of praying. The life of Christian prayer calls us to submit to a long and costly process of sanctification — of dying in the old self-centered life, and so being reborn into that new kind of life and selfhood which is of God.

5

God's Freedom and Man's

GOD DIFFERS FROM man, not only in degree, but also in kind. The life of Christian praying is never the relation of equals. The relationship of God to man in praying has about it always something astounding and surprising. We see this distinctiveness clearly in the difference between God's freedom and man's.

God's freedom is the only true and perfect freedom. His freedom is not the freedom of choice, such as is ours. St. Augustine has aptly expressed this difference:

> It is already a great freedom to be able not to sin. But the greatest freedom consists in the inability to sin.

So long as we are at the mercy of choice, we are not truly free. True freedom is not freedom to do either right or wrong, but the power and will to do only that which is true and right. God's freedom consists in his joyous and full ability and will to be and to express all that he wills, to live at the level of eternal life.

But the freedom which sinful man has is of a very different kind. It is the freedom of choice, even though the choice may be so imperceptible to our conscious minds as seemingly not to exist. Our freedom of choice also involves the risk of mis-choice. Blinded as man is, and handicapped and imprisoned in self-centeredness, how can that which man calls his freedom be any real freedom, when he lives by his own clouded wisdom, not God's; and by his own frail goodness, not the steadfast goodness of God?

Rather must man learn to renounce voluntarily and gladly this freedom he calls his own; otherwise he cannot enter into that perfect freedom which God means him to have. We are to hope and look forward to that day and state when we shall no longer have any choice. Our will then will have but one purpose — to do God's will. So often men do not know this single purpose of life here upon earth. Men wonder and ask why they are here. But when we waken to and accept the one central purpose of life — that we are made for God, for his glory, and for intimate fellowship with him — then all of earthly life will take on a new and radiant spiritual meaning and joy. Only when we are set free from the many, conflicting desires within us, by renunciation of the old self-centered being, can we then enter into that new God-centered selfhood, in which we are truly free to manifest the life of God here upon earth.

Perfect freedom comes to us paradoxically only when we give up our distinctively human kind of freedom and gladly and willingly submit our lives to the full sovereignty of God. The language of devotion here gives expression to this paradox, as theology cannot do, in its ancient Collect: ". . . whose service is perfect freedom . . ." We shall be truly free to be sons of God only when we have voluntarily renounced all that freedom which we have called our own, and which is self-centered; and when we accept joyfully that loving, spiritual servitude to God, under which we shall know true and perfect freedom. We can then enter into that new life with God to which alone can rightly be given the name of sonship. How can servitude also be sonship? That is one of the very deepest of religious paradoxes. The paradox is not resolved by reasoning, but by entering into that double experience of loving servitude and sonship.

With Jesus the conception of God's fatherhood carried primarily not the thought of protection and sentiment, but of a Father's will to be lovingly obeyed, no matter what cost it might involve. We of the West have often failed to grasp the Oriental conception of fatherhood, and have forgotten that Jesus was an Oriental. The obedience of Jesus was an obedience lovingly and gladly given to God, his Father.

Always in our praying we are to remember that our will is confronted with God's will. In the conflict between those two wills, his never budges. It is our will, and not his, which must bow and yield. The life of Christian praying is our learning to surrender more and more fully and completely our will to his will — joyfully, willingly, lovingly — that he may be truly sovereign in our lives. In so doing we enter through loving obedience to God into a new kind of freedom, unknown to the world, and in which all that we do issues from truly Christian love for God and for man.

God's Love and Man's

In the life of Christian praying we grow into a deeper and deeper realization of the important distinction between God's love for man, and man's love for God. Without our awareness of this important distinction, our praying so easily misses the amazing note of God's prevenient relationship with and to us. God's love for us is the prevenient love of the Creator-Father for his creatures. More than this, it is his love for us creatures who have again and again turned our faces away from him in rebellion; who have forgotten and ignored him; who have taken his manifold blessings and gifts for granted, counting them our own by right; who have betrayed him, grieved him, and sinned grievously against him.

His love for us is not simply a love for us, if and when we are righteous. None of us dare claim to be righteous before him. God's love for us is a love given to us while we are still sinful, unrepentant, selfish, blind, proud, ungrateful. His love is not a love given only to the worthy, calculatingly measured in accordance with our merits and deserts. Rather it is a love given wholly for our sakes; utterly unselfish and wholly self-giving, holding nothing back, and seeking nothing for himself. It is a love concerned only and always for our true welfare and redemption. We can only look upon his love for us in utter amazement and wonder. It will always come to us as something unexpected and wholly undeserved. How can he, the Holy One, love us, the sinful and the foolish? His love always confounds us and humbles us.

But our love for him is a very different kind of love, even when it is distinctively Christian and at its highest level. Our love for him is not even to be compared with his love for us. For we, in loving God, are loving One who has always done us good, and never betrayed us, forgotten us, or abandoned us. He is all-worthy of a far greater love than we can ever give him. Our love for him is comprehensible: it is only what we owe God. Thus there will always be a great and important difference in kind between his love for us, and ours for him.

All of us need to awaken to the realization that not all love from man to God is distinctively Christian. So much of our love for God is essentially selfish, self-centered, and self-seeking. It is our attempt to use God for our own profit and gain; to make him serve our sins. We turn to God because we feel some lack or need, and we hope to get from God that which we desire simply for the mere asking. We live as if God were made for us, instead of our being made for God, for his glory. When we do not live for God we find that life does not go so well; we are prey to fears and restlessness. Joy and radiance come to us only when we live for God. But our love for God, when at last it becomes truly and distinctively Christian, will have a very different motif from that of use: it will be the love which springs not from need but from thankfulness.

A most important linguistic fact of the New Testament has not yet received the attention which it merits from scholars. It is the distinction between the New Testament Greek word ἀάγπη (agape) and the non-Christian Greek word ἔρος (eros). In the world into which the early Christians went, the current and widely used Greek word to express man's love for God was ἔρος. It is therefore most significant that when Christians sought to give expression to their Christian love for God in the New Testament, they never even once used this word ἔρος. They knew with uncanny accuracy that Christian love for God from man is a very different kind of love from ἔρος love. Whereas ἔρος love is essentially self-seeking, they knew that Christian ἀγάπη love from man to God is essentially self-giving and thankful.

Christian love from man to God is always rooted and grounded in the prevenient love from God to man, even while he is still sinful. As John expressed it: "We love him, because he first loved us." Christian love for God, ἀγάπη, is not rooted primarily in man's needs or desires for himself, but in man's joyous thankfulness for that which God has already done for him, and in loving obedience which flows from such a mood of thankfulness to God. It is a love for God which has as its aim, not man's profit, but solely God's glory. It is our loving doing of God's will.

Thus in the life of Christian praying we on our part awaken to the need of thoroughgoing and perpetual purgation of our deep-seated and hidden motivations. There is very much in every one of us which must be changed and which must die, before we can become wholly God-centered. Only so can that new life of the spirit, with its distinctively Christian love for God, be born in us and grow strong and stable. And more and more shall we awaken to the mighty and amazing wonder of

God's ἀγάπη love for man, that love which saves us from self-centeredness and gives us the spiritual freedom which is true freedom.

* * * * *

These basic and fundamental convictions concerning God and man are all-important and significant for the distinctively Christian life of praying. The One to whom we pray is the initiator of praying, for he is the prevenient Creator God. He it is who raises us from death into the risen life, which is eternal life. Our proper relationship with that God is the relationship of creaturehood, acknowledging and joyfully accepting dependence, obedience, thankfulness, and living a life of which the center is always God.

Our actual status is that of those who have rebelled against God and are sinful. We have sought to be our own God. We are lost and must be found. We need a Saviour to save us not from circumstances but from ourselves. We require the long, persistent working in us of the Indwelling Spirit, lovingly and patiently breaking down every resistance and leading us into the death of self and into new birth of the spirit. In our temptations and sinnings we turn to One who is untempted and sinless; we surrender our false freedom in order that we may enter into that true and perfect freedom of the "sons of God," which is our Father's will for us. As we gain insight into the important and saving distinction between God's love for us and our love for God, we are born into that new life of love for God which is distinctively Christian.

Having laid these foundations for praying, we now turn to God's Christ, that from him we may learn how to pray in adoration, in self-giving, in intercession, and in thankfulness; how the praying life is nourished and deepened; how in the power of Christian praying we may learn to deal victoriously with temptation and sin, and persevere against all obstacles; and how we may, through the mighty disciplines of praying, become teachers of praying to our fellow men: so that both they and we may at the last come to the fullness and perfection of the life of Christian devotion.

PART III

"Our Father"

Our Father:
> Thy name be hallowed;
> Thy kingdom come;
> Thy will be done.

How can we better learn about praying that is distinctively Christian than by turning to Jesus Christ, who is the Lord of prayer?

Jesus ever sought to know and to do his Father's will. To that will his whole life was unbrokenly and unswervingly dedicated, given gladly in holy and loving obedience. In his life we behold a life at all points truly human and devoted with complete and perfect self-giving to the hallowing of his Father's name, to the coming with power of his Father's kingdom, and to the unswerving doing of his Father's will. In Jesus we are given by God a life seeking nothing for himself, but ever living for others, offering himself wholly and perfectly to his Father "for their sakes." His was the one, true, pure, and perfect interceding life, because he was wholly set free from any service to himself. His, too, was a life dominated from beginning to end by thankfulness, able even in the heart of adversity to turn to his Father and cry, "Father, I thank thee."

Jesus' whole life was a life of praying, for with him life was prayer and prayer was life. In him we find adoration, self-giving, intercession, thankfulness in their perfection and rooted in his Father's will. Only as our lives become consistent with our praying, and our praying consistent with our living, and as we, following Jesus, manifest these spiritual qualities in our lives can we truly fulfill Christ's purpose in giving us the prayer in which he commands us to say, "Our Father."

6

Praying as Adoration

GOD SEEKS IN the life of praying to turn us away from our preoccupation with ourselves. For we are imprisoned in self-centeredness. The center of our life is to be transferred from ourselves to God. God accomplishes this by leading us into the life of adoration.

God has given to all of us rich experiences in the realm of adoration. We can readily remember moments in our lives when we stood in the presence of a wondrously beautiful sunset; under the starlit sky; before the breath-taking beauty of the rainbow; or upon the peak of some lofty mountain. At the moment we did not think or reason. We were content simply to stand and behold. When later we did reflect, then we found these facts to be true.

We remembered that in the moment of beholding we became quiet and still. Our chatter ceased, even if only for a moment. There was deep quiet, within and without. We remember also that at such moments we mysteriously and peacefully forgot ourselves. So absorbed were we with what was outside ourselves that we ceased to think of ourselves. That which was outside ourselves became central; we, peripheral. Again, we noticed that the mood of claiming and demand died within us. Before such great beauty and glory we ceased to ask or desire anything for ourselves. We had no desire to own it, to keep it, to change it, to use it. For the time being we escaped from the slavery of the kingdom of "means-to-an-end" and lived joyously in the kingdom of ends themselves. We joyfully and spontaneously called others to share in the experience: — "Quick! Come! Look!" We found ourselves possessed by the mood of utter unselfishness. It was an experience of adoration.

In these moments of adoration there came a "centering," a unifying, a grasping of something tremendous, something at incalculable distance yet seemingly near at hand, in its wholeness and perfection. We were not torn between this and that detail. Everything centered in but one thing, seen as a whole, and each part took its proper place in the whole. We saw intuitively and wholly. We did not reason or analyze. A sense of peace and of cleansing pervaded our whole being. We realize now, as we look back upon those moments, that the action started primarily from outside ourselves and acted upon us; our role was one of spontaneously giving ourselves over, completely passive, open, and receptive. It acted; we watched. It gave;

we received. This is the mood which is called adoration.

At first we do not relate these experiences of nature adoration to God. Nevertheless it is through them that God prepares us for the experiences of religious adoration, which come later. Then we realize that there is a very close relation between the experiences of nature adoration and religious adoration. Moreover, once we have been awakened to God, we shall find in and through the moments of nature adoration the much deeper levels of religious adoration for which the other is the preparation. The division which we make between the "secular" and the "sacred" exists only in our limited thought and not in reality. From God's standpoint all is sacred. As we truly live in Christian praying, we too shall learn that nothing is really secular, unrelated to God.

God wills us to turn to him in the mood of adoration. When we approach God as adorers we look steadfastly upon him and so forget ourselves. For it is to adorers that there can come from God those deep and wondrously satisfying insights which are the marks of eternal life, that life which starts even here in this earthly life.

Adoration involves a meeting between God and man: an act of revelation on God's part, and a humble and disinterested response on man's side. Too infrequently does this word "disinterested" enter into our religious vocabulary. We mean by it something very different from uninterested. We use it to describe a turning to God, which is free from all traces of any self-seeking. It is a centering in God, and not in ourselves.

There is help at this point also in the analogy of coming to know a person. There are many stages of knowing a person. With some people we have only a nodding acquaintance. We are able to identify them and recognize them. Even at this surface level of meeting we perceive something of their inner, invisible, spiritual state — based upon their casual mannerisms, their behavior to those they like or dislike, their appearance, tones of voice, etc. Within definite limits, all this is real knowing.

From other people comes to us what is primarily a "hearsay" knowledge, dependent upon the reports and observations of others, which also reveal to us much of the inner state of those making the reports. But such knowledge is at best a second-hand knowledge, which may never develop into direct, first-hand knowledge unless we make the opportunities for eliciting these data.

With still other persons we have, even after years of acquaintance, only an external knowledge. We know their conduct well, so far as externals go, but we know little of their motives. We know the books and papers they read, their likes and dis-

PRAYING AS ADORATION

likes as we see them at work or at play. We have talked much with them, but their conversations do not reveal their inner life. We can be with them over the years and still confess that we do not really know them.

But there are some persons of whom we have the much deeper knowledge to which we give the name of friendship and love. Sometimes friendship and love are born out of many years of acquaintance; sometimes out of a single meeting. Thus we say that "we fall in love." How, knowing so few facts about the other, two people can enter into this deep love for each other, we cannot say. We only know that it does happen. With such people we have the sense that the friendship and love is something which comes to us and seizes us. It comes to us as a gift.

With God, too, we may have these varying levels of knowing. There are many who have but a nodding acquaintance with him, lasting only as long as the nod. There are many more — far more than we readily admit — whose only knowledge of God is about him, second-hand; and who never arrive at the first-hand knowledge of him that comes from first-hand experience with him. We all start our religious life by leaning upon the experience of others. The child's first knowledge of God is not direct, but rooted in the belief and practice of parent and teacher. It is possible to go through adult life without ever passing beyond this second-hand knowledge of God. There are also very many whose only religious knowledge is that of the externals of religion. Their interest and main concern is with the minutiae and mechanics of church life. This constitutes a deadly temptation for many of the clergy. Here the externals of religion — "churchiness" — become the substitute for knowing God. But it is also possible to have with God that deep and rich relationship, which is his friendship and love, and which the New Testament calls eternal life. It is only this kind of knowledge that can ever satisfy the heart of man and set him at rest and at peace. The life of praying seeks to prepare us for that kind of knowledge of God.

When we meet a person or a thing, a self-disclosure is given to us. Most of us experience it and grasp it first in the realm of our relations with nature. Understanding it there, we can then relate it to God's action, in which he gives us the revelation of himself.

When we reflect seriously and deeply upon our relations to nature, we realize that there is always much more to nature than we have as yet grasped. All knowledge to date is at best only partial and incomplete and therefore tentative knowledge. We are convinced that there still lie hidden in objects of nature a richness and a meaning to which we have not as yet awakened. It is this conviction that underlies the persistent research work of the physical scientists. The true scientist is confident that there are still a myriad more secrets to be revealed in nature, and he therefore goes back again and again to basic material, hoping to receive new insights, new impressions, new data, some of which will prove to be "fertile seeds."

We know that in the realm of nature some men are able to see, hear, touch, smell, taste more than others. Some persons are more sensitive to the revealing action of nature than others. Thus the bird lover will spot birds and will hear their calls where we cannot. The geologist will read the wondrous story of the earth's history in the fragments of rock and sand, where we ourselves see nothing meaningful. We look at the same visual data, but we perceive not their meaning. To be able to receive their significance requires a sensitiveness and familiarity bred of much humble attention and a freedom from self-preoccupation.

The witness of such people is evidence to us that in the natural world there is much more reality than we ourselves have yet plumbed. We overlook much. The sensitiveness of the scholar, the artist, the musician, the saint challenges our insensitiveness; their seeing, our blindness; their hearing, our deafness. There is much that we could hear and see and love, but do not. The difficulty lies not in the object withholding its secrets, but lies rather in our refusal to fulfill the basic conditions of increasing constantly our capacities for further and deeper receptivity. All of us need to give a more sustained and loving attention to what is around us, and so intuitively to enter more deeply into the heart of nature and people. Our knowledge need not ever remain superficial and shallow. Our knowledge of persons and of things can, if we will, develop into deep insights, which eventually are spiritually saving.

God is ever seeking to reveal himself to us. But his self-revelation can only be received by those who are humble, docile, patient, obedient, and receptive. Just as within the realm of the natural sciences knowledge is given only to the disinterested, the truly open-minded, the alert, and to those who unselfishly love that with which they are dealing, so too in the realm of the spirit it is required that we draw near to God often, humbly, lovingly, ever aware of the mighty gulf which exists between the Almighty God and the tiny creature — self. Only so can we receive from God the revelation which is a large part of fellowship with God, and which he is ever preveniently seeking to give to us. Ultimately we can draw near to God in but one of two moods: the mood of using God selfishly, or the mood of disinterested love — the mood of adoration.

PRAYING AS ADORATION

The vivid analogy of family life can perhaps help us to grasp this truth. Probably every parent has had the experience of returning home after an absence, to be greeted at the door by his children, crying out: "What have you got for us, Daddy?" It is a very natural and common greeting. Some of us have also had another very much more meaningful experience — that of having a child greet us with: "Oh, Daddy, I'm glad to see you."

Such words, uttered spontaneously and with love, are very different from those same words, used in later adult life as a conventional greeting. In one case the child's reaction is rooted in a hope and delight in a gift for himself. In the other, there is a disinterested delight in being with the beloved one himself. Out of these common, human analogies there can be given to us, if we are humble, deeper insights into our relations with God.

We shall approach God then, either as beggars hoping and desiring to receive gifts from him; or as adorers primarily concerned not with what profit we shall gain, but with sheer and unselfish delight in God himself. In moments of adoration, we shall have no thought or concern for what we shall get from God. Only afterwards do we awaken to the fact that gifts from God came to us — the unutterable gifts of his love and friendship. But they came to us unsought. We did not adore him in order to get gifts. Rather we adored, and over and above the adoration for its own sake, there came to us rich gifts of God.

All of us are very prone to traffic shamelessly in our human relationships. We use one another's name and reputation, influence and position in order to secure our own gain. We know that whenever the mood of using or being used creeps in, friendship begins to die. From those who approach us with the intent to gain something for themselves, we tend to withhold our deeper selves. We reveal our inner life and give ourselves spiritually only to true friends, who draw near to us in disinterested concern.

With equal shamelessness we are prone to traffic for selfish gain in our relations with God, and when we do so, we shut out God, and also we are shut out from receiving the deep and rich fellowship which God wills to bestow upon us. For God would have us approach him not as beggars, but as adorers. When we adore him disinterestedly, he reveals himself to us far beyond our greatest imaginings. As adorers we establish with God very different relations than we do if we approach him as beggars. When we approach him coldly, calculatingly, selfishly, how can the revelations of his unselfish love be given to us, and how can we receive them? To the adorer God becomes friend and companion, and then reveals himself.

Our moments of adoration are at best fleeting and intermittent. They are not subject to our command. They come suddenly and unexpectedly. But we remember them as moments of great and abiding joy. Long after the actual moments of adoration have ended, we find ourselves living upon their strength and inspiration. We have faith and hope that life holds out to us the promise of more and even deeper moments of adoration for the future. The adoring life is a large part of eternal life.

On the contrary, our most unhappy and miserable moments are those in which we have been possessed by the mood of claiming, and are concerned primarily with ourselves and our myriad and insatiable desires for ourselves. At such moments we are aware of what we want and have not; or of what we have, and want not. The fruit of these times is always discontent and complaint of some sort, and takes many different forms.

Our basic need is to have our attention turned outward and away from ourselves — turned toward God. For God has not made us for ourselves, but for himself. We can therefore never find our true peace and happiness when turned inward upon ourselves. God has created us for himself, for his glory, for fellowship with himself — a fellowship of unselfish loving. This is according to the law of creation. When we awaken to it and obey it, we enter that true sonship with our Father, which is marked by loving and holy obedience. In these matters we learn best by trusting our lives to others with greater faith and spiritual wisdom than our own. As we do so, we find that experience corroborates our trust. Then we know for ourselves, first-hand, of this great law of creation.

God has to face in us deep and serious resistances. Down through the ages man has become deeply entangled in and enslaved to many things and persons, which seek to claim him and hold his attention. Each of us knows what it is to be so attached to and absorbed in human friendships, possessions, work, that very little if any time and energy is left for God. Our work, our families, our churches, our communities, our pleasures, our basic needs of food and clothing and shelter can easily use up all of our time and energy. Because we have relegated God to the non-secular life, we have not learned to find him in and through all of these earthly realities, although he is there.

We live as if we were made for ourselves. We forget that we were made for God, for his glory, for fellowship with him. Perhaps we have never known, because we have never been taught, that we were made for God. But God will not let us find any rest or peace in any person, thing, or in ourselves. He means to teach us that we are made for him, and for him alone. Nothing will go well or be able to satisfy us until we enter into relations of true fellowship with him.

In later years we look back upon our spiritual history and give God thanks for the long process by which he loosed us from all these persons and possessions to which in our blindness and selfishness we had become so firmly tied. At the time we did not detect in this work of detachment the hidden, mysterious, powerful, persistent action of God. Only after years have passed and the work is well advanced does he awaken us to his work, and only then do we begin to co-operate with him. He works in us in myriad, hidden, and mysterious ways: in times of sickness, in the breaking of our earthly friendships, in the betrayals which have left us lonely and hurt, in the many disappointments, in the countless experiences of restlessness, in the death of those dear to us.

In all of these experiences, which come unsought by us, God is working decisively. In his great wisdom and patience he knows best how to work in us. We learn slowly that we can never be successful while seeking to escape his presence and resisting his action. We may flee him, but he never turns back from accompanying us; and at the end of our flight from him, we find him awaiting us. In every event he prevenes us and seeks to win our free following of his leading. To him our hearts are wide open, every desire known, and there are no secrets which we may hide from him. How very often he is the reality working in and through the disturbing and discomforting thoughts which come suddenly to our minds. They do not come to us by chance.

In the life of Christian praying we heed and seek to obey these mysterious workings of God. We learn slowly that much depends upon our immediate and willing obedience to them. When we do not live by the light of prayer, we often seek to ignore them, to forget them, to resist them, to disobey them. We have thus a very decisive part to play in this work of God for, in, and upon us. We give our free consent to God's action in us. We work with God, even to the extent of being for God and against ourselves; or we work against God, which means that then we set our little wills against God's mighty and unbending will. We shall find that the universe of God will not budge before us, when we set our wills stubbornly against all the mighty powers of God's ordered world.

In the life of Christian praying we joyfully and peacefully give God the time and attention and consent which he asks from us. Thus does God work his redemptive action in us with every resistance broken down. But in this work we shall have to fight against long-established tendencies to forget God, to ignore him, and to live for ourselves as if he did not exist. We shall have to fight against deep and hidden fears of the inevitable, worldly consequences of belonging wholly and first to God.

A passage from the spiritual writings of Fénelon aptly expresses this battle within us:

> Man wishes to serve God, but on condition of giving him only words and ceremonies, and still more, short ceremonies, of which he is soon tired and wearied. Man wishes to love God, but on condition that he love along with him, and perhaps more than him, all that he does not love . . . Man wishes to love him, but on condition of not diminishing at all this blind love of himself, which reaches even to idolatry . . .
> God does not admit any contract with us, except that which belongs to our first allegiance with him in baptism, where we have promised to renounce everything in order to be his; and in the first commandment of his law, where he exacts without reserve all our heart, all our spirit, and all our strength. Translation of *Réflexions Saintes,* Jour XXVI, Tome 18, pages 67–8, Lebel Edition, 1823.

In Christian praying we joyfully desire to give God our attention as adorers. We find it the very deepest joy and freedom to give our attention so solely to him, that we completely forget ourselves. True, our natural tendency to approach God for our purposes and needs, will again and again break in upon these times intended for adoration. But we are not to become discouraged at the persistence of this counter mood of use. When we become aware that adoration has given way to use, we at once, quietly, turn again to God in adoration and seek to adore God for what he is. Slowly but definitely over the years these times of adoration of God drive out from our lives any self-seeking.

Slowly and imperceptibly the mood of adoration is built up in our lives. At first we may find ourselves self-conscious in our acts and words, but bit by bit they take hold of our lives and we enter into spiritual peace and joyousness. Soon adoration becomes natural to us, and we do it spontaneously, without effort; and we learn of its mighty creative power.

Our moods are normally created by the doing of oft-repeated, short acts, which by themselves seem very insignificant, but which over a period of time accumulate to have a truly great power over our lives. For every willed act into which we voluntarily and intently throw ourselves has the mysterious power of transforming us. We slowly and imperceptibly become very different persons. In praying we enter upon a steady, untiring discipline of living, which will make adoration not dependent upon chance or event — so sure to fail — but which will make adoration a stable mood.

7

Praying as Adoration (*Continued*)

WE SEEK TO make adoration steadfast with loving regularity. The acts of adoration are very simple, but their work is great.

The form in which we express adoration is so important, we shall now give it our attention. In soliloquy we converse with ourselves. The form of soliloquy is therefore inept for adoration. In adoration we look steadfastly at God, not simply at our own thoughts about God. In Psalm 103 we have the example of a man talking to himself about God, rather than talking directly and disinterestedly to God:

Bless the Lord, O my soul; and all that is within me, bless his holy name.

Bless the Lord, O my soul, and forget not all his benefits.

This is the mood of reverie or reflection. But compare this with another Psalm, which is adoration:

> I will magnify thee, O God, my King;
> And I will praise thy name for ever and ever.
> Every day will I give thanks unto thee;
> And praise thy name for ever and ever.
> Great art thou, O Lord,
> And marvellous worthy to be praised;
> There is no end of thy greatness.
>
> PSALMS 145:1-3 alt.

The most natural form for adoration is that of direct address: not "God is," but, "Thou, O God, art." The form "God is" really belongs to instruction. It is the form of theology, not of praying. We are not yet sufficiently aware of this important matter of form, either in praying or in worshiping. Many of the hymns and prayers used in public worship are couched in the form of indirect discourse. They are about God, rather than directed to God. This is not to say that there is no place in public worship for language about God. But there are parts of public worship in which the form should most certainly be that of direct address, if the worshiper is to be led into the practice of the presence of God.

So much of the material of the *Psalter* and the *Hymnal* benefits the user greatly when it is transposed into the form of direct address. This principle can be well seen when applied to the fine, ancient hymn of St. Patrick. (372-466 A.D.) The indirect form in our hymnals reads:

PRAYING AS ADORATION

I bind unto myself today,
The power of God to hold and lead,
His eye to watch, his might to stay,
His ear to hearken to my need.
The wisdom of my God to teach,
His hand to guide, his shield to ward;
The word of God to give me speech,
His heav'nly host to be my guard.[1]

The direct form reads:

I bind unto myself today,
Thy power, O God, to hold and lead,
Thine eye to watch, thy might to stay,
Thine ear to hearken to my need.
Thy wisdom, O Lord God, to teach,
Thine hand to guide, thy shield to ward;
Thy word, O God, to give me speech,
Thy heav'nly host to be my guard.

So, also, in the case of the Song of Mary, the mother of Christ, which we are accustomed to sing or recite in the third person; the original experience of Mary before uttering it for Elizabeth must surely have been expressed in direct address. The indirect form reads:

My soul doth magnify the Lord,
And my spirit hath rejoiced in God my Saviour.
For he hath regarded
The lowliness of his handmaiden.

[1] Tr. Cecil Frances Alexander, 1889. Words by permission of Arthur C. H. Borrer, Executor for Mrs. Alexander.

For behold, from henceforth
All generations shall call me blessed.
For he that is mighty hath magnified me;
And holy is his name . . .

The direct form reads:

My soul doth magnify thee, O Lord
And my spirit hath rejoiced in thee, my Saviour.
For thou hast regarded
The lowliness of thine handmaiden.
For behold, from henceforth
All generations shall call me blessed.
For thou that art mighty hast magnified me;
And holy is thy name.

Similar gain is to be had in taking the indirect and theological expression of the early Christians' faith, as contained in the Apostles' Creed, and for the use of personal devotion, recasting it into the form of direct address. Originally the Creed was used as the baptismal symbol, and the adult candidate for baptism recited it to the congregation. That fact alone explains why it is in the indirect form. It was not at first used as a profession of faith toward God. But when it is used, as we are now accustomed to use it, as an expression of our personal faith in and to God, it might then well be recited in the form of direct address. It would then read thus: —

I believe in thee, O God:

> Father,
> Almighty,
> Maker of heaven and earth:

And in thee, O Jesus Christ:

> Only Son of God,
> My Lord and my Saviour;
> Thou who wert conceived by the Holy Ghost,
> Born of the Virgin Mary;
> Suffered under Pontius Pilate,
> Crucified, dead, and buried;
> Thou didst descend into hell;
> The third day thou wert raised again from death;
> Thou didst ascend into heaven, and
> Art seated on the right hand of the Father;
> From thence thou shalt come to judge the living and the dead:

I believe in thee, O Holy Spirit;

> And in thy holy Catholic Church,
> The communion of thy saints,
> Thy forgiveness of our sins,
> Thy resurrection of our life, and
> Thy gift to us of life eternal. Amen.

At first thought, it may seem to make little if any difference to change from indirect to direct address. But when we reflect upon the change in form, and humbly practice the direct form of address, we shall soon learn its very real significance. When we say of a human friend, "He is," it implies the absence of the person of whom we are speaking. But when we say, "You are," it always implies the presence of the person. So too in our praying, the use of the direct address will gradually deepen in us the awareness of the presence of God.

These great, historic Christian affirmations concerning God make ideal forms for prayers of adoration. Recited and prayed daily over the years, slowly, lovingly, humbly, they deepen and quicken in us belief in them and commitment to them. By so using them we learn slowly to identify our lives with these great and mysterious acts of God to which he has committed himself.

The first part of the Lord's Prayer itself makes a perfect prayer of adoration, for in it our concern is in no way for ourselves, but wholly for God:

> O Heavenly Father:
> Thy name be hallowed;
> Thy kingdom come;
> Thy will be done:
> On earth as it is in heaven.

These familiar words take on as many shades of meaning as the moods in which we utter them.

Much of the biblical material, when used for personal devotion, gains greatly by being recast into the form of direct address. In a true sense, it is our return to the basic and original experience which lay behind the verbal expression of it to others. At first we shall need to use the affirmations of others and trustfully lean upon their deeper faith in God, until slowly over the years we are given by God himself our own living, strong faith in God. At the end of this chapter we give a number of very simple biblical prayers of adoration, to serve until you find the particular forms which give expression to your own adoration of God.

Prayers of adoration are usually short and not wordy. Thus they do not require much actual clock time. In fact, most of them will be found to be almost instantaneous. No life is so full and busy that it has no time for acts of adoration. They do not require a book, a church, a place of solitude, or kneeling. They are essentially outward manifestations of interior and invisible adoration. The acts have a dual purpose — to express and also to impress. As the Baron von Hügel said: "I kiss my child because I love it, and I kiss my child in order to love it."

At first it may seem artificial to engage in words of adoration when one is not possessed by the mood of adoration. But once we perform the act and say the words, we quickly enter into their reality and their power and find them to be truly expressive. We find that a rare quality of spiritual joy and peace comes from truly disinterested praying. Loving regularity of adoration will exercise a truly creative power in our lives, and we find the center of our being slowly transferred from self to God.

Once we learn to pray as adorers, we look back and realize how much we missed in not living in the life of adoration in the past. This note of unselfish, unasking love for God usually comes rather late in the spiritual life. But to realize from the very beginning that it is one of the high peaks of the Christian spiritual life will encourage us to expect its coming, and enable us to interpret it when it does come. We are to realize that we have not yet reached our goal until our life reaches the level of constant adoration. Eternal life is essentially adoration.

In seeking as beginners to enter the Christian life of praying we discipline ourselves into making our very first waking thought each morning one of adoration. Those who have not yet formed this habit will find it difficult at first to remember it, and it may seem artificial. But once we find ourselves joyfully and effortlessly turning at once to God upon waking, we no longer need conscious effort and constant reminders to do it. When occasionally we miss this waking act of adoration, we feel that an integral part of the day is lacking.

God has brought us to the beginning of each new day. All through the sleeping hours, when we could not watch over ourselves, he has been keeping watch over us and restoring us. We waken into the new day in his presence, and the first fitting act of each new day is to acknowledge the presence of God. "This is the day which Thou hast made. We will rejoice and be glad in it." To turn at once upon waking to God in loving adoration will mean for us a very different day than if we begin it by turning in upon ourselves as center, taking up yesterday's still unsolved problems or presuming to pierce into the unknown future. By turning at once upon waking to God we begin each new day by entering once again into intimate, joyful, loving, non-asking, disinterested companionship with God.

The essential adoration is the turning from self to God in adoring love. The words can be as simple as these: "Glory be to Thee, O Lord," or, "I praise Thee, O God; I acknowledge Thee to be the Lord."

Spontaneously upon waking we find ourselves turning in the mood of adoration to God, and we start each new day with the companionship of God. our Father. When we give ourselves to the life of adoration we soon, with God's providence guiding us, find ways and means to remind ourselves upon waking to adore God.

Disciplines can have helpful power in religion, as in other phases of life, so long as we use them wisely. The fact is that the religious life cannot be made dependent upon inclination, desire, or mood.

Often there are days when we have no spontaneous, natural inclination to adore God. For such days we all need the helping hand of regular disciplines, reminders to ensure that we do perform the rightful acts. Discipline can be a much more firm and stable foundation for the life of praying than either feeling or will, provided that the discipline has been initially rooted in Christian theology and is intended strictly not as a goal in itself, but as a means toward reaching God.

The mood of adoration will never become stable and powerful if it is limited simply to this waking act. The mood of adoration gradually and definitely expresses itself in frequent, short acts scattered throughout the whole day. It is very easy to forget God throughout the day, as we busy ourselves with our daily work. We do not begin by finding God in and through all things. We have slowly to learn to find his presence in this thing and that person, and then bit by bit we find him in more things and persons, until at last we have such a sustained sense of his constant presence that we walk with God throughout the whole day, and we walk with him as adorers. It is hard for us to think of him as absent. It is much like the experience of falling in love. The beloved one is constantly in our thoughts and imagination. Even when we are so busy that we have no conscious thought of her, we know that she is in the background of our consciousness. We need short and oft-repeated acts of adoration to help us to remember God's perpetual presence. Our tendency to think of God as distant and aloof needs to be replaced by the deep biblical conviction that God is intimately concerned with everything that we do.

For most of us our days consist of a series of short acts, linked together by time. Much of our daily routine is at least semi-automatic: dressing, eating, walking, driving, doing chores. These duties seldom require our full and undivided attention. This means that our minds are left free in the midst of much of our activity to turn for an instant to God, and remind ourselves of his perpetual presence. It is in these times of busyness that God comes to meet us and to give us his companionship.

Every one of us has some short act which we perform many times a day. We can associate with these oft-repeated acts the practice, as an adorer, of remembering God and turning to him in adoration. The great French spiritual directors of the seventeenth century used to tell their people to turn their minds and hearts to God each time that they heard the clock strike the hours. We of today might well mark a small symbol — a cross — upon the face of our wrist-watch, so that whenever we looked at our watch we would be reminded to turn to God in adoration. We might make a similar usage of the traffic lights. Many times daily we have to wait a moment while the traffic light remains red. Let us use these times of waiting to adore God. Gradually we form the practice of turning to God in loving adoration hundreds of times each day, and thus keep a more frequent companionship with him.

His presence and his companionship become more and more real for us as we practice these short, oft-repeated, inner turnings to God in adoration. God becomes the most real of all realities, more real and living and close than any other thing or person. We find ourselves adoring him so often that it becomes for us as natural and effortless as breathing. We are becoming God's "remembrancers." Out of this keeping of continual companionship with God there issues a growing and deeper knowledge and love of him. Slowly and after many years of faithful, loving adoration, we find that our life becomes truly centered in God. Less and less is our primary concern for ourselves and for our own needs and problems. More and more our lives become God-centered.

But we must expect that self-centeredness will die in us only slowly and with deep resistances. Again and again the mood of demand and subtle self-seeking will break in upon the mood of unselfish adoration. But over the years the battle is slowly won, and our lives enter wondrously into the spiritual love, peace, power, and joy of the fellowship of adorers.

At the beginning of each today we have an act of joyful, loving adoration of God. Then repeatedly throughout the day, in the midst of all our busyness, our heart and mind turn for an instant to God in joyful adoration. As the last act of the day again we turn to the ever-present God and commit ourselves to him. So do we fall asleep — into that untroubled sleep that every adorer of God knows. To commit ourselves to him in adoration is to drop every earthly care, knowing that his loving providence watches over us. From adoration we pass into sleep, to awaken the next morning again to take up the joyful life of an adorer of God. Always we are to remember that all of our adoration has behind it the prevenience of God. We adore God, because he has given us the will and the desire to adore him.

Prayers of Adoration

1. Holy, Holy, Holy, Lord God of Hosts,
   Heaven and earth are full of thy glory,
   Glory be to thee, O Lord Most High.

   Sanctus

2. Blessing, and glory, and wisdom, and thanksgiving, and honor, and power, and might, be unto Thee, our God for ever and ever. Amen.

   REVELATION 7:12 alt.

3. Great art thou, O Lord, and marvellous, worthy to be praised; there is no end of thy greatness.
   PSALMS 145:3 alt.

4. Thine, O Lord, is the greatness, and the power, and the glory, and the victory, and the majesty; for all that is in the heaven and in the earth is thine; thine is the kingdom, O Lord, and thou art exalted as head above all.
   1 CHRONICLES 29:11

5. We praise thee,
   We bless thee,
   We worship thee,
   We glorify thee,
   We give thanks to thee for thy great glory,
   O Lord God, heavenly King, God the Father Almighty.
   Gloria in Excelsis.

6. Thou only art holy,
   Thou only art the Lord;
   Thou only, O Christ, with the Holy Ghost,
   Art most high in the glory of God the Father.
   Gloria in Excelsis.

8

Praying as Self-Giving

AS WE GIVE ourselves more and more fully and deeply to adoration of God, we find that adoration develops imperceptibly into self-giving. When we adore, we want to give. What we want to give is not simply external gifts, but ourselves. Self-giving is inseparable from truly Christian adoration. Self-giving is our progression from self-ownership and self-will into the full sovereignty of God. It involves the renunciation of self-centeredness and self-seeking; and also our being born of the spirit into new selfhood, organized about God's will.

Unfortunately praying as self-giving is not known or practiced by many people. Because of this unfamiliarity with it, we need, before considering the acts of self-giving, to gain a true and adequate understanding of what God is seeking to do for us in leading us into such praying. What is God's purpose in it? What assistance and what resistance do we offer him?

God has created us for himself, for his glory, and for fellowship with himself; not that he is seeking something for himself, but that he is seeking us for our sakes. This means that we cannot then live for ourselves, or by ourselves. If we attempt to do so, the whole order of God's universe is set solidly and unbendingly against us. This friendship with God, which is his purpose for each of us, can come to us only as a gift from God. Never is it something which we earn or win or achieve by ourselves, without God's prevenient action. Every attempt on our part to achieve this friendship with God, relying upon our own efforts alone, is in substance presumption and lack of humility. God, not man, sets the conditions of this intimate fellowship and it can be had only by conformity and obedience to those conditions.

To have friendship with God involves necessarily the transformation of our old self-centered being by God's own action in and upon us into the likeness of God. We do not start our life in the likeness or image of God, as we have already seen in the earlier chapter, "Immortality or Eternal Life by Resurrection?" To say that we must become like God in no way implies that we can escape or ignore the basic distinction between man and God. Even in heaven man will ever remain a creature, utterly dependent for both the fact and the kind of his existence upon the Creator God.

In God there is no trace of any self-seeking. His whole life is characterized by never-ceasing self-giving, in order that his creatures may be blessed and saved. It is because his life is so utterly and completely self-giving that spiritual joy is a dominant note of his life. "It is more blessed (spiritually joyous) to give than to receive." God knows this truth, and he wills that we too shall enter into that same wondrous spiritual joy. There come moments in our lives when we too experience indubitably the truth of this great law of life. Faced with some great need in another's life, we find that we gave ourselves lavishly and without calculation, with no thought of what might be entailed for ourselves, in time, energy, or possessions. In those moments we knew deep and abiding spiritual joy, quite different from all secular joys. Into this joyous life of self-giving God wills us to enter. One of the major purposes of the life of praying is that God shall engraft into our lives, which by nature are so much characterized by the very different spirit of self-getting, his life and spirit of utter self-giving.

As early as we come to know ourselves we find our lives already strongly self-centered. Thus focussed on our own selves and our own possessions, our lives are in a state of disorder and consequent unrest. These outward and visible manifestations of restlessness are the symptoms of an inner malady, which is essentially a lack of any rootedness of life in God. We also know that we are somehow misfits in a universe of divine order. This awareness comes to us as we gaze at the undeviating order of the stars in the night sky. When our lives follow the undeviating order of God, then we too shall accept our appointed place under God and know both in our own lives and in our relations to others that deep and stable peace of God which passes all human understanding.

We know that we have become so deeply attached to things and to persons and to ourselves that we have no longer power to detach ourselves. We gradually learn that not we ourselves, but God, is the main factor and agent in the long, progressive work of detachment. For it is God alone who sees and knows fully the nature and danger of our earthly attachments, to which we are so often blind. He sees, as we cannot see, the danger of inordinate and possessive attachment of husband and wife, of parent and child, of friend and friend.

When we awaken to the incomparableness of the fellowship that God offers us to that which we now have with our fellow men, we shall realize that only as we cease to cling possessively and inordinately to the human friendships can we begin to enter into the wondrous and joyful spiritual fellowship with God, which will then bestow upon us a new spiritual fellowship with our fellow men, far deeper and richer than we ever had before with them. Then we shall accept the deep truth of our

PRAYING AS SELF-GIVING

Lord's own words: "He that loseth his life shall find it; he that keepeth his life shall lose it." There is then a major place and emphasis in our life of praying for this detaching action of God and for our response of giving full consent to God.

Because so many have never been taught what is the central purpose of man's life on earth, they often wonder why they are here. But once we have heard and accepted this Christian purpose of life — that we are made for God, for his glory, and for intimate friendship with him — then the whole of life here on earth takes on a new and satisfying significance. But however great may be our confusion or bewilderment concerning the purpose of our lives, God knows completely the purpose of our existence. He has brought us into existence for his purpose, and he sustains us in order that that purpose may be fulfilled. We know ourselves only in a very fragmentary and partial way. We know ourselves as spirit far less than we know ourselves as body. But God acts upon us with complete and perfect knowledge of every factor, whether we think it relevant or irrelevant to him. He knows what we require: often we do not. His action is limited and conditioned only by his self-subjection to the ways of divine love.

God can make us creatures without our consent. He cannot make us sons and friends without it. God's work upon us for his purpose is both negative and positive, detaching and attaching. He has myriad ways of detaching us from all that absorbs us and becomes a rival to himself. God is a jealous God. But we are not to interpret the divine jealousy in terms of our human jealousy, which is always self-seeking. God's jealousy is never for his sake, but for ours. He knows how much we are missing when we seek to live apart from him. He is jealous because he wills to give us the high gifts of holy friendship, and he cannot tolerate our lives becoming so attached to earthly realities, good as they may be, that we have no time or concern for spiritual fellowship with him. He knows that we can never be truly joyful until we place him first in our lives, and thus enter into that holy friendship with him which is the pearl of great price. Therefore God must be jealous — yes, even angry and wrathful — at the idols which absorb us in earthly life.

Through the death of friends and loved ones; through sufferings permitted or sent to us in God's providence; through the failure of our schemes, plans, and hopes for self-aggrandizement; through our experiences of boredom, loneliness, and restlessness; through sickness and accidents: through all these experiences we center our whole attention on the effect not upon others but upon ourselves, and we are so far from being God-centered that God acts to detach us from ourselves.

But God is also working positively to attach us to himself. He attracts us through his gifts of many forgivenesses, which operate in us even before we awaken to them in repentance; through his dim and mysterious leadings of us in our darkness; through his presence and conquering power in times of temptation and sinning; through the power of the words and deeds of his Christ, coming to us when we worship and pray, or as we study him; through the saintly friends given to us by God to teach and encourage us on our way; through the spiritual love, peace, joy, and power which ever flow from instant obedience to his still, small voice within us; through the never-exhaustible grace given to us in his sacraments. Out of all these experiences our lives have been knit by God to himself in the bond of unutterable gratitude. Gratitude has led to acts of loving self-giving to God. But such times of self-giving to God are apt to be spasmodic and temporary, and soon they get neglected and then forgotten. If they are to become creative and to bear much fruit, they cannot remain isolated acts but need to be repeated and stabilized, and so become a mood and temper characterizing our whole life. Repeated self-giving to God, ever deepening gratitude for his myriad blessings to us, gradually becomes a dominant mood of the truly Christian life.

But this purpose of God to attach us to himself

and thereby to detach us from possessions, from people, and most of all from ourselves, meets with very strong resistances in us. Deep within each of us is the powerful and deeply ingrained desire and will to own and manage our own lives. We want to have and to do our own will in all things. We see this clearly in the life of the Apostle Peter. Peter's determination not to allow Jesus to wash his feet along with those of the other disciples, as being an act beneath the proper dignity of the Messiah, was rejected by Jesus. Peter then seeks in a more subtle way still to have his own will performed. He asks that Jesus shall wash, not simply his feet, but also his face and his hands. He seeks to have Jesus act according to Peter's will. And Jesus again has lovingly but firmly to deny this to Peter, as being the last resort of a stubborn self-will. How often we, like Peter of old, insist that God work in our way and in our time.

By the time that each of us reaches the years of adulthood, long years of self-making and self-will lie behind us with their rigid power. Self-will starts early in childhood. A little child turns to its parent and cries out with strong determination, "I don't want to take your hand. I want to go by myself." The adolescent years are full of ample evidence of the strength of self-will, the desire to rule one's own life prematurely and to become more and more independent of all parental control. They are dangerous years of self-making. The cross-currents of conflicting wills only serve to make self-will the more rigid.

Having reached the stage of self-rule, each of us is then confronted with God's call to surrender the self-made and self-centered ego into his hands, that it may die and the new Christ-made self, centered in love and in obedience to God, may be born and grow in us. Gradually, almost imperceptibly at first, but persistently, God calls us to give ourselves wholly and unconditionally to him. For many years, and even decades, we may deafen our ears to this inner call, but God will never abate his steady pressure upon us. Sooner or later each of us comes to our day of decision, in which we accept God's call. To accept God's call means embarking upon the stormy waters of inner warfare.

Even when we acknowledge and accept the truth that we are to give ourselves to God, we insist that it be within limits, and within limits set by ourselves. Thus from the time of ancient Israel down to our own age it has been taken as the counsel of perfection that God is entitled at most to ten per cent of our wealth. The remaining ninety per cent is by right man's own. One wonders what God, who gives without limit, thinks of man's carefully measured weighing out of tithes, of this very ancient and persistent estimation as to what he is entitled. There is too little awareness even today that this really constitutes rank blasphemy. Jesus teaches his disciples that all that we have and all that we are belongs by right to God. Self-giving is not Christian until it is the giving of all. All is God's, and we are entitled not to own, but only to use, and use for his purposes. God, who gives all, demands all.

Down through history man has been offering to God substitutes for this giving of self. Mankind has been willing to offer costly possessions to God in the hope that thereby he might win God's favor. He has given of his sheep and oxen, his grain, his wine, his money, his time. He has given his children. But still God is not satisfied and man knows not peace. Thomas à Kempis has rich and rare wisdom to offer us here:

> Whatsoever thou givest besides thyself I regard it not; for I look not for thy gifts, but for thee. For as it should not suffice to thee to have all things besides me, so it may not please me, whatsoever thou give, unless thou give *thyself*. Offer thyself to me and give thyself all for God, and thy oblation shall be acceptable. *Imitation of Christ:* Bk. IV, Ch. viii.[1]

Mankind again and again seeks to enter into contractual relations with God. Man would strike a bargain with God, with carefully stipulated con-

---

[1] From *The Imitation of Christ*, Thomas à Kempis. Whitford-Klein version copyright, Harper & Brothers. Used by permission.

ditions which are binding as much upon God as upon man. "If — then — " But God does not and will not bargain with us. He will not let us have any choice or voice in setting the conditions of fellowship with him. He seeks a relationship of friendship and sonship. He demands total, blind, unconditional giving of self to him.

At first man fears what may be involved in such total, blind, and unconditional self-giving to God. What does God have in store for us? What will happen to us, if we thus renounce self-will and self-ownership? We already know enough of religious history to know what has been involved for others who have so entirely given themselves to God. We remember Jesus, and that his utter self-giving and unswerving obedience to his Father led him to the cross. We remember that Paul's self-giving led him to scourgings, stonings, beatings, imprisonments, and finally to a martyr's death at Rome. For Father Damien in our own day and age it involved leprosy. We know instinctively that God's ways are not our ways. We know that his way is the way of the cross; and that it is bloody, costly, and involves suffering. We naturally shrink from such full commitment to his way. From our side we see only what it takes away from us. We cannot see from God's side all that it will bring to us.

But did Jesus ever regret having given himself to his Father in loving and holy obedience? Did

Paul finally bewail the surrender of his life to the risen Christ on the Damascus road? Did Father Damien wish that he had never seen that leper island in the Pacific? We know beyond all doubting that these found in the doing of God's will their own joy and peace. "In thy will is our peace." But much must happen to each of us before we can make our own the words of John Henry Newman:

> I was not ever thus,
> Nor prayed that thou shouldst lead me on;
> I loved to choose and see my path;
> But now lead thou me on.

For many long years we desire to belong both to God and to self, so slowly do we learn that we cannot belong to God and to self. The choice is God *or* self.

As we come to know God's wondrous love for us and for all mankind, we find ourselves giving ourselves freely, wholly, blindly, unconditionally, joyfully to him. Our whole life becomes more and more a thank-offering. We enter into the spiritual joy of self-giving and we offer ourselves gladly to do God's costly work of redemption.

The pattern for Christians for giving themselves to God is that of Christ's utter self-giving. God's Christ literally emptied himself, and accepted to the full in becoming incarnate the cost of such self-giving to his Father for man. On earth he offered his body to be broken for us. He offered his blood to be shed for us. Dare we to follow in his footsteps and offer our bodies and our blood that they may become his body and his blood, and that he may break them and pour them out at his will for the salvation of our fellow men? Dare we entrust our lives to his wisdom, power, light, mercy, love? Or shall we continue to walk by the dim sparks of our own little, earthly wisdom? "Lo, I come, O Lord, to do thy Will." We need more of that kind of praying.

God creates this mood of self-giving in us, if we are willing to have it and if we will use it for his purposes. All of our acts of self-oblation are only our surrender of ourselves to his sovereignty. We throw ourselves into repeated acts of self-giving, ever at deeper levels, that God may take from us ourselves and make us wholly his. This is the basic purpose for our existence and for our prayers of self-giving.

Once we understand and accept this purpose of God for us we find ourselves wanting to engage in the daily acts of self-giving, which over the years will bring about in our lives a stable mood of oblation. Just as in Christian marriage the husband and wife, who day after day replight their troth to one another, with each day's plighting reach to ever deeper levels of love and unity so too those of us who give ourselves day after day wholly and unconditionally to God find ourselves having ever more and more to give to God.

Each day, directly after our waking act of adoration, we offer to God ourselves — all that we have and all that we are — in holy and joyful obedience to his will. We say:

> O God, I give thee myself this day:
> To hallow thy name,
> For the coming of thy kingdom,
> To do thy will.
> Take me from myself, and use me
> As thou wilt,
> Where thou wilt,
> When thou wilt,
> With whom thou wilt.

It is essential that the form of the words indicate total and unconditional obedience. Often they must be spoken even in fear of consequences and against inner resistance. Such praying is work of the most difficult kind. It is sheer labor. There will always be, down to the end of life, much that we do not want to give to God; as also much that we do not know must be given. It is like a parent who sees a little child playing with a discarded double-edged razor blade; he asks the child to give it to him, but the child only clutches it the more tightly, and will not give it up; then, for the sake of the child himself, the parent firmly has to pry open the clutching fingers and take it from the child. So it is also in our resistances to God's taking away from us all our self-centeredness and self-possessiveness. We need therefore an additional act of renunciation, in order that God may take from us that which we will not voluntarily give to him, or which we know not must be given. A great prayer to God the Holy Spirit expresses this:

> Come, O Holy Spirit, come:
> Come as Holy Fire, and burn in me,
> Come as Holy Wind, and cleanse me,
> Come as Holy Light, and lead me,
> Come as Holy Truth, and teach me;
> Convict me,
> Convert me,
> Consecrate me,
> Until I am wholly thine.

It is only God who knows what we must part with, and how and when it is to be taken from us. We ourselves do not and cannot know. Therefore we place this work entirely in his hands. We on our side will offer no conscious resistance to him. Whatever he wills, that we are ready for. We entreat him to act, even against our will. Fénelon writes thus of this action: "I am for Thee, against myself." It is a strong prayer, but we require such a prayer.

When we thus pray, God does act. We expect him to act, and we find that future events work out his action in and upon us. The events of history serve his will. We begin to enter upon that mysterious and costly, yet also joyful and peaceful process of self-oblivion and self-renunciation. We learn bit by bit that far more than a mere patching up of our lives is required. Nothing short of complete eradication of self-centeredness is the prerequisite of our being "born again" into that new life of the Spirit, which is characterized by being truly God-centered. We are to fall into God's loving, wise, powerful hands. We are to take our hands off of ourselves and to let him act.

This work of praying is so all-important that it requires being done repeatedly throughout all our days and years. Knowing by faith that God's providence rules over all the events of history, of each today and of all that it holds, we go humbly and trustfully into each event that the day brings to us. When temptation strikes, we accept it humbly as permitted by God for our testing, as being necessary and best for us, and as being offered to us by God for our gaining of deeper self-knowledge. When sickness comes to us, we do not seek to resist it impatiently, but rather we enter fully and willingly into its hidden mysteries, confident that some purpose of God can be worked out in it, both for ourselves and for others.

When people betray and deceive us, or hurt us, we quietly and silently turn to God and put our whole trust and confidence in him. When loneliness comes to us, again we turn to him, remembering that the purpose of all loneliness is to turn us to his never-failing companionship. When we yield to temptation and fall into sin, we learn more deeply of our need for God, and again we turn to him and entrust anew our life to him for his remaking, knowing that his mercy and forgiveness are inexhaustible. Thus in every event of the day, we first of all turn to him, give ourselves anew to him, and then with God go into and through whatever may be the experience of the day. When the day is over, we turn again to God, offer it all to him, and give him thanks for it. When we come to the chapter "Praying as Thankfulness," we shall be dealing with that deep mystery of giving God thanks even for adversities.

Over against this mood of accepting all and entering fully into every experience will be the natural mood of desire to escape adversities and to resist them. But in so doing we shall miss their hidden meaning and blessing from God. Let nobody call the response of prayer an escape from reality, an easy way. Nothing is more real and difficult than to meet all events with God, and to enter fully into them; and so to receive through them the manifold blessings of God. Far from being pure passivity, this really involves a state of determined and labored activity on our part.

We know that nothing can happen to us without the full presence, full knowledge, and full redemptive concern of God. In every event of our lives, even in our sinning, God enters redemptively into the experience and acts, whether we accept or resist his help. He is always adequate for every circumstance. We place our faith in his action in every circumstance and event, and as Christians give him our humble and loving obedience, even when we walk in the darkness. When we do so we find that he never fails us. We offer our lives to be God's apprentices. We know that we have much more to learn and to endure if we are to live, not under our own blind sovereignty, but under God's holy and wise providence.

Then finally, as the closing act of each day, just before our act of unselfish adoration before going to sleep, we turn to the ever-present God, and gathering up all that the day has held for us, we place it trustingly in our Father's hands. We take our hands off completely. It is an act full of reposeful, spiritual joy, pervaded by the mood of work done and ended, which is now brought to God as an offering.

This act of gathering up and placing all our actions in God's hands is an act which will accomplish much more than any efforts we can ourselves make to examine them, judge them, or correct them. We are not in any way seeking to escape responsibility for our actions during the day. Even though we might want to avoid them, they cannot be escaped. God will not permit that. But by bringing them to God, we thereby acknowledge and accept full responsibility for them.

We know that their judging, correcting, and mending require a wisdom and purity of heart far greater than our own. We entreat God to deal with these our acts, and with us, in his way and in his time. Often there is no good reason why we should at once know the full significance of our acts of today. More often years must pass before we are able to bear and to see and to profit from the fuller light of God thrown upon them. Then suddenly, when least we expect it, God himself awakens us to a much deeper realization of what we have done. Then, too, God shows us the historic consequences of our past acts, to which we have been so blind; and also something of what he has done to them and to us.

This kind of praying is one of the keys which unlocks the doors which lead into the kingdom of God's peace, joy and power, which far surpass all our little human understanding. We learn over the years to commit each today trustfully to God, knowing that he and he alone is sovereign Lord of our lives and of the world. We do not make bold to take upon ourselves those works for which only he is adequate. We remember that it is he who is

God. We are but little creatures. We then no longer try to control the past. To deal with the past redemptively is a work far beyond our little powers. That work is his, not ours. By self-giving we learn to live more humbly, and more peacefully.

9

Praying as Intercession

CHRISTIAN PRAYING is more than an individualistic relationship with God. Adoration and self-giving require also to be supplemented by truly Christian intercession. God has a purpose in leading us into the mystery and power of intercessory praying, and our first concern is to seek to understand that purpose of God.

As we grow into the life of Christian praying, we gradually arrive at the great Christian conviction that God cares, and cares redemptively, for each and every one of his creatures. The very thought of this staggers all of our human powers of comprehension. When we seek to deal with vast numbers of anything, we can only do so by dealing with them in generalities and abstractions. We soon lose sight of uniqueness and individuality. But we ought not to be surprised that the ways of our heavenly Father far surpass our limited worldly understanding. We rejoice that we have Christ's own proclamation that the Father cares for the individual sparrow and that he has numbered the very hairs of our head.

Our eyes become opened to the realization that the cross is the perfect symbol and shape of God's care for all of his creatures. So often we see in the cross only the reminder of the death of Jesus. Yet it can mean much more than this. It can express to us the deep mystery of the descent of the transcendent God into intimate immanence with man; as also the wondrous fact of God's all-embracing, all-inclusive love for his whole creation.

We can learn much from the use in the *Book of Common Prayer* of the word "all." For there it is the adjective most commonly used, apart from the adjectives describing God himself. Normally we use an adjective to narrow attention down to a certain aspect of a thing, in order that we may center attention upon that aspect. We thus use adjectives to exclude and shut out from our attention that which we do not at the moment wish to consider. But the adjective "all" is one of a small class of adjectives which goes counter to this rule. We gradually learn that the adjective "all" is a distinctively Christian word. It embodies the all-embracing and all-inclusive spirit of God himself. But it is only slowly over the years that we learn through adoration and self-giving that caring is not Christian caring until it is caring for all.

In the life of Christian praying we find our lives entered into by God himself, seeking to ingraft his own spirit of caring for all. He invites us to enter into the wondrous joy of his own life — the spiritual joy that comes only to those who live for others, and forget themselves. We see this note vividly and unforgettably pictured for us in the life of Jesus.

On his last journey from Galilee to Jerusalem, we would naturally expect that Jesus would be so preoccupied with his coming death at Jerusalem that he would have no time or concern for the needs of others. We can understand the action of his disciples in forbidding parents to bring their little children to Jesus to be blessed. The disciples could not accept Jesus' repeated warning of his approaching death. They had just been given the reassurance of his Messiahship. To their minds it was utterly inconceivable therefore that Jesus could be put to death. To them the going up to Jerusalem meant the inauguration of his kingdom. With these matters upon Jesus' mind, they could not possibly understand his taking time to give attention to insignificant children. We rejoice to see how Jesus does take time to sit down, take children into his arms, and bless them.

Even when they had traveled as far as Jericho, the last halting place before climbing up to Jerusalem, and when death lay so close ahead, again we notice how Jesus gives himself as always to the work of bringing others into fellowship with his Father. We, who have known loneliness and despair, can realize the surprise and joy of Zacchaeus, as he hears Jesus asking to be his guest over night.

On the night when Jesus was betrayed in the Garden of Gethsemane we see with utter amazement his complete unselfishness, and his deep and abiding care for his disciples. Thrice in the midst of that agony of temptation, he forgets himself to go to the three sleeping disciples, to watch for them. We cannot believe that he goes to them to get help from them for himself. We remember that only an hour before he had foretold that this very night all of them would forsake him and flee; and that one of them, Peter, would this very night deny him. We watch him turning to God in prayer for help and strength and light for the doing of his Father's will. His going to the three sleeping disciples therefore was not for his own sake, but for their sake. In that one long hour of agony of waiting for Judas to come, we see him thrice concerning himself with the danger and needs of his three disciple-friends.

Finally upon the cross, in the midst of all the pain and anguish of actual crucifixion, we see Christ occupied not with his own bodily and spiritual suffering, but instead with the blindness and darkness of those who had crucified him. We hear that amazing cry, "Father, forgive them; for they know not what they do." We remember that one of the taunts directed against him while upon the cross was this, "He saved others; himself he cannot save." No, he cannot. He was so busy even then saving others, that he had no time even to think of saving himself. As we ponder and wonder at his life, with its utterly amazing unselfishness, we begin to gain some dim understanding that very much must happen to our lives, if we are to be conformed to his life.

As we now actually are, our lives are marked by the note of selection, limitation, and exclusion. Our vital concerns easily are limited to those whom we naturally like, and to those to whom our lives are knit by the ties of kinship and proximity. We like our exclusive clubs and societies and communities. Even our churches imperceptibly and subtly become exclusive and snobbish.

The life of prayer is always fraught with the danger of turning inward upon ourselves and of becoming self-centered, selfish, and even petty. Therefore, because we need a strong antidote against self-concern and self-petition in our praying, we voluntarily enter upon the discipline of never praying for ourselves, except in relation to our self-giving to God, or in our relation to the needs of others. This discipline may at first sight seem too radical and even impossible, but there are very few of us who do not need it if we are to be set free from our ingrained and deep-seated self-centeredness and enter into that new God-centered life, where self is forgotten and therefore at peace. Actually we shall never be able entirely in this life to escape some self-praying, but we can assure that self occupies a less and less central place in our prayers.

Our very best praying for ourselves is the giving of ourselves to God — wholly and unconditionally. We find that under his sovereignty we are fully and perfectly free. If we pray the prayer of self-giving, we then need no other petitionary prayer for ourselves. The practice of not praying for ourselves, but incessantly interceding for others, will bring much fruit to our praying. God wills that we shall be set free from the service of ourselves, which is slavery, in order that we may then give ourselves more fully and perfectly to the work of adoration and intercession. Thus our lives become truly cruciform. The bars of the Christian cross really have no ending; they extend on and on with their redemptive concern. Upon each arm of the cross we are to see an infinity sign. Such is to be the pattern of our lives.

The basic motif of intercession is simple to grasp. We turn to God and offer to him our strength, love, energies, time — our whole life in its entirety — in order that God may use them in his providence for the blessing of some other person. Intercession is thus truly Christian praying, because in it we give ourselves to God for another, seeking nothing for ourselves. Behind whatever words or acts we use there is to be, at the heart of all our intercessions, this basic desire that another life shall come into the relationship with God which saves; and for that end we offer to God all that we are and all that we have. In Christian intercession we seek nothing for ourselves, but only the glory of God and the salvation of another person.

There are many in the world who do not pray for themselves and who have no vital concern for God. There are many who have not as yet become awakened to God and to the wondrous joy of his friendship. There are many who have nobody to pray for them, until some of us undertake to fill the role of intercessor for them. We have relations with many people, but we say to ourselves that others pray for them and therefore it is not our obligation. The result is that many are not prayed for at all. The Christian Church intends to be a great fellowship of intercessors, dedicated to the vast work of interceding for all, so that none be left unprayed for. In intercession we link our lives with Jesus himself, who ever offers intercession for all of us.

In order that all men may be saved, and that they may enter into that holy fellowship with God for which he has created them and sustains them, we turn to God and offer to him our energies "for their sakes." It is the same deep passion which dominated Paul and which he expressed in his letter to the Christians at Rome, "My heart's desire and prayer to God for Israel is that they might be saved." We, with our limited freedom, may not be able to enter into another person's inner life, but God in his perfect freedom and prevenience can work in and upon the person's life with the energy and love which we have offered.

In the life of prayer we find that there comes to our minds the thought of various persons, and with it the dim but real impulsion to intercede for them. We obey this inner leading of the prevenient God, and offer ourselves to him for this work of unselfish intercession. Our natural tendency, when we would help another person, is to engage at once in some external action directly related to that person. But in Christian praying we are invited to use a more excellent way — to turn first of all from the person we would help and to go to God who alone can truly help him. Our first act of intercession will be that of turning to God and our second act of intercession will be to offer our life to God for him. We say: "O God, I give thee myself — all that I am, and all that I have." And then: "Take me and all that I have; purge and cleanse it, and use it as may be most for thy glory and thy blessing of. . . ."

God entrusts very definite and particular persons to each of us to intercede for, just as he entrusts us to definite persons who pray for us. For we little human beings just cannot carry all of mankind. That role is far beyond us. But there are definite persons with whom God has knit our lives in his providence. To all of us he has given father and mother. To many of us he has also given husband or wife, and children. To all of us are given friends and fellow workers and immediate neighbors. For all of us there are at least a few "friction" people given too; those with whom we find it difficult to get along, those who trouble and annoy us and whom we should very much like to get away from and ignore and forget. As Christians our lives are knit to a particular local church and to a particular minister. We live in a specific town or city and in a definite state and nation. For these persons and groups we are particularly to intercede. They are the people whom God would have us "carry" in prayerful concern.

Great benefit comes in making our intercessions pointed in intention. It is not that general prayers are not valid or helpful. But we can never sufficiently remind ourselves that God's concern is for each individual creature and not simply for people in masses. In public worship of necessity the prayers of petition are general, but here we need to remember their historic origin in the Church. At the time of corporate intercessions, the deacon would ask for the prayers of the congregation. He would request their prayers for Anne in sickness, for Peter in prison, for John traveling. Then in silence each worshiper would offer to God his own love and energy for that particular person. Only then would the deacon "collect" the mood of them all and express it in a generalized prayer. But in our personal intercessions we do well to direct our prayers specifically for definite persons.

We do not need to use written prayers, nor a book of prayers, nor memorized prayers. Love knows how to give utterance to its concerns. We speak lovingly, simply, directly, and in our own words — stammeringly and falteringly perhaps at first. The words are not for God's sake, but to articulate our thoughts and desires for us. God reads our hearts and knows our desires and thoughts long before we express them in words. All that we need to do is to turn our hearts toward God; name the person; then offer to God our loving and unselfish concern for him.

If we use the prayer which Jesus has given us, we then pray "in his name" for people. This one prayer asks everything that is necessary and best for them. All our myriad desires and hopes as Christians are truly gathered up fully in this one prayer. No other prayer that we can devise can ever compare with it. This prayer was given to us by the Master of praying. We use it for intercession by putting the name of the person into each clause:

Our heavenly Father:
> Thy name be hallowed in Richard,
> Thy kingdom come in him,
> Thy will be done in him today,
>> As it is in heaven.
>
> Give Richard today his daily bread;
> Forgive him his trespasses, and
> Teach him to forgive all who trespass against him today;
> Let him not succumb today to temptation,
> But do thou deliver him from all evil.

It can be further simplified in this way:

> Our Father:
>> Behold thy child Richard:
>> Feed him,
>> Forgive him,
>> Lead him,
>> Save him this day.

What is it that we pray for when we intercede for another? It is not that our will for that person be done, and not that we shall in any way benefit ourselves; that would be turning intercession into self-petition. Intercession, as we have already seen of adoration, is essentially disinterested, unselfish praying. The moment that any trace of "for our own sakes" creeps into intercession, it ceases to be distinctively Christian. Our one central concern in Christian intercession is that the person prayed for shall know God and be saved, thus fulfilling God's purpose for that life.

At first, until the work of Christian intercession becomes well disciplined and as natural as breathing, we find help in writing out a list of those for whom we believe God means us to intercede. For whom would God have us intercede? That is a far surer question to ask of ourselves than the more natural one, "For whom do I want to intercede?" Make God's list and then place it in your Prayer Book or Bible or notebook. The list naturally includes:

Father and mother
Wife or husband
Children
Friends
Immediate neighbors
Minister
Town or city
Nation
Particular persons in need: sickness, anxiety, etc.

Why does God want us to intercede for people? It is not because alone he cannot accomplish the salvation of these people, but in order that they and we may have spiritual fellowship both with him and with each other. God's will is not simply for individualistic salvation, but for a Church — a fellowship of the redeemed.

The actual intercessions for these need not be made all at one time. They can be spread over the whole day. We can make them anywhere and at any time, for this is essentially secret action. We do not require a church building — helpful as that can be — nor quiet, nor kneeling, nor a minister, nor a book of prayers. All that we need is a Christian concern born out of God's concern for persons. We can intercede while driving our car or waiting at a street corner for a traffic light to change. While people about us are aimlessly chatting, we can mentally engage in this work of intercession.

God also links our lives with strangers, whom we know not by name and whom we may never meet again; we are walking on the street and notice the strained and anxious face of a person who passes by; we notice the fatigue written in the face and posture of the man seated across from us in the train; we see a person under the influence of alcohol; we overhear another's vile language: for all of these strangers we offer unselfishly to God our loving intercession, that they may be saved by God. We accept humbly and willingly the divine injunction to be our brother's keeper, not just for him, but for God.

We do not need to see or fully understand how God uses our offered energies. Our belief in the power of intercession is rooted primarily in our faith, responding to the prevenience of God. God is Father, and he cares redemptively for every man. We cannot believe that when we turn to him and unselfishly offer our love and energy for one of his needy creatures, he will pay no attention to our offering. Does God care less than we do? We have faith that God takes whatever we offer to him for others, purges it, directs it, and uses it in his mysterious providence for the blessing and saving of that person. This is not however to claim that he uses it just as we expect or desire, but only that he uses it in his wisdom and love. As we practice this intercessory work over the years, we are given by God himself to know and see something of the mighty power of Christian intercession upon the lives of those for whom we pray.

All of us have more time to engage in this intercessory work than we utilize fully. We all have time which we can use while traveling from home to office; from home to store to do the marketing and shopping; the time we spend in day-dreaming. These times we can use for this joyful, fruitful work of intercession.

Intercession has a mighty power even in instances where the person prayed for knows nothing about it. Perhaps most of our intercessory praying will be done without the person's knowledge. It may happen that after years of intercessory praying by somebody for us, an incident ordered by God's providence awakens us to the fact that another has been praying for us. There is the instance of the saintly Marie Rousseau, an obscure and humble widow of a Parisian wine-seller, accosting the worldly Jean Jacques Olier one day on the streets of Paris and informing him that for three years she had been daily praying to God for his conversion, that he might undertake under God the much needed work of reforming the clergy of Paris. This same Olier later became the founder of the famous Seminary of St. Sulpice in Paris, where he was to teach the young men studying for the ministry that a major part of their training lay in the hidden souls in France, who were unselfishly interceding to God daily for their ministries. To inform a soul prematurely that we pray daily for him may be pride and self-seeking on our part and call forth an attitude of deep resistance from him. But when after years of daily praying for another we feel impelled to reveal it, we are to do so. Our intercessions are not to be limited simply to those whom we know, but to reach out to strangers we happen to meet along the way, or about whom we have heard.

But our intercessory concern is not to stop there. It is also to reach out into that very near but invisible world, which we call heaven. For we can live not simply in this earthly world, but also in heaven. We need not postpone our heavenly living until after death. All of us have dear ones who have entered through resurrection into that other world. Shall physical death terminate our loving concern for them? Do they have no needs — spiritual ones — for which we can still offer our energies and love? Is there not spiritual growth for them there? Is there still not much evil even in the most saintly which must be purged from their lives? We remember St. Augustine's request of all those who read his *Confessions*, that they pray for his mother Monica in that other world. And shall our prayers for the dead always be only petitions? May they not often be rather of the nature of thankfulness?

Do we really believe in the credal conviction of the "Communion of Saints"? Do we believe that they in the resurrected life have no concern for us and no fellowship with us who still live upon this earth? Have we no concern for them there? How shall we ever come to enter into the truth and richness of this Christian conviction unless we actually pray for them and so learn the truth of this deep Christian faith?

We believe that death and resurrection by God bring us a deeper and truer vision of God and of our own selves; that they give us a full awakening to what we have made of ourselves in this earthly life; and that they confront us with the need of voluntary submission to God's purging of every trace of selfishness and sin from our lives. Who of us in the moment of death would presume to claim that we are ready for full and permanent fellowship with God — eternal life? Life there, because of the awakening that death and resurrection bring, must of necessity be a richer, fuller, and truer life than that which we live here on earth. We have the deep faith therefore that those who have already gone into the resurrection life see their lives and ours in much truer light than we can. They have a new and deeper concern for us than we have for ourselves. There is much that they can do for us. We have the faith that their eyes behold us in all that we do. That alone can be for us a real deterrent in times of temptation. Out of our concern for them and theirs for us can be born a deep, personal, and Christian fellowship.

That there have been tragic abuses made of this great Christian conviction in past ages, we do not deny. It is true of all great realities that they are easily misused and trafficked in wrongly. But besides abuse and misuse there is also right use. Fénelon gives us the true corrective:

> . . . People who are not at all familiar with diamonds, or who do not look at them closely enough, can take an imitation for a fine gem; but it is none the less true that there are real

diamonds, and that it is not impossible to recognize them. *Spiritual Letters:* page 15.[1]

There is a truly Christian concern for the dead, as also a selfish and pagan concern for them. So long as we seek God's will for our dead and offer our love and energy to God for him to purge and use for their blessing, we need not hesitate to intercede for them.

So many of us have been awakened by God over the years to the incalculable debt we owe spiritually to great men and women of God, whom we have never known in the flesh. Yet they have acted upon our lives through the veil which separates that world from this, to be our great teachers of God. Through their books and through the impact of their lives upon history, our lives have been deeply affected and influenced. We find ourselves having a living fellowship with them through the veil, and we joy in their companionship. We have firm support for this practice and faith in the Gospel records of Jesus' life. Jesus had so deep and rich a spiritual companionship with Moses and Elijah that on the Mount of Transfiguration he could have the experience of real converse with them. He knew that they were following with deep interest and intercession his ministry, and especially his coming death at Jerusalem. For a moment the veil which normally hid the "dead"

[1] From *Spiritual Letters of Fénelon.* Copyright, 1945, Idlewild Press. Used by permission.

from the living was lifted. So too we may have, as gifts from God, rich and blessed companionship with the departed.

This work of intercession has very real consequences. The first and foremost result is that it actually conforms us to God's redemptive concern for all. We find our lives sharing more and more in his love for all. We find ourselves living less and less for ourselves, and like God, living more and more for others. We find that we are given by God deeper and truer insight into the real needs of those for whom we intercede. We enter into richer and fuller companionships with people, just because they are rooted in praying.

Moreover intercession is a great source of health and purity of life. There is a marked difference in power and cleanliness between a mountain stream and a stagnant pool. The mountain brook never stays still. All that it receives from on high, it at once passes on. The stagnant pool receives, holds fast, and will not give out freely. It thus becomes dirty and foul. So too it is with our lives. The selfish life holds fast and will not give out in intercession. The intercessory life at once gives out and passes on to others all that it has received from God, in order that others may thereby be blessed and saved.

But there is also a real and objective power upon those for whom we intercede. God takes the energy and love which we offer to him and uses it to bless and save others. Behind every man's salvation lies hidden much Christian intercession. Often God uses us indirectly for the salvation of another person. Sometimes he uses us directly, for when we pray unselfishly for another, God often gives us concrete opportunities of implementing our praying with action. We are also given through intercession a much deeper insight into the essential meaning of the Church — that great fellowship of all those whose lives are knit together by God in Jesus Christ.

Occasionally God in his great mercy allows us to discover that some person has been interceding for us over the years, while we were unaware. We awaken then to the knowledge that all along we have been living upon the energies offered so unselfishly by others. It is a very humbling awakening. At once we are impelled to accept the obligation and joy of pouring forth to God from our lives all that he has given to us, in order that others may be blessed and helped as we have been.

The life of intercessory praying is an integral part of the life of every truly Christian husband and wife. For Christian marriage, among other things, is the acceptance by both parties of the awful responsibility for the spiritual welfare of each other, that through their marriage the other may be led into deeper fellowship with God, that fellowship for which marriage is man's truest and deepest image. If every husband knew that each day his wife said the Lord's Prayer for him, as he for her, there would be built up over the years the very deepest and most abiding foundations for Christian marriage. For that which is prayed for in the Lord's Prayer includes all that is highest and best. No divorce could occur if husband and wife lived truly the life of Christian praying.

And with the coming of children in marriage, as the gift of God, again there needs to be full and deliberate acceptance by both parents of spiritual responsibility for the children. Not simply their physical well-being, or their worldly success and security, or their health; but first of all their fellowship with God: that is the primary purpose of parenthood. No work in life is of so much importance as this one of leading a child into friendship with God. The Christian parent prays daily the Lord's Prayer for each child; and then as the children grow in years they too can be led to pray the Lord's Prayer for father and mother. In Christian homes the parental relationship to children is firmly rooted and grounded in intercession.

Intercession brings an exceedingly deep, spiritual joy to our lives, the joy of God himself in his unselfish concern for all of his creatures. To enter into that spiritual joy is part of the great and high purpose of God for our lives. It is an integral part of eternal life, to which God is calling us, and in which we live for God, for his glory, and in intimate fellowship with him.

10

Praying as Thankfulness

WHEN WE UNSELFISHLY adore and give ourselves wholly and unconditionally to God, and intercede for our fellow men in Christian love and concern, we find that our life becomes radiant with thankfulness. The more we adore, the more we thank God not merely for all that happens to us, but for himself. The more we give ourselves to him the deeper is our gratitude at being under his wise and loving providence. The more we intercede for others the deeper grows our thankfulness for Christ's Church — that great interconnection of lives which together form his body upon earth. But Christian thankfulness is distinctive and very different from the ordinary, everyday thanksgiving of those who live apart from God. Christian experience always takes the ordinary and lifts it up to the level of God's Christ, to give the experience new and deeper meaning and glory.

Thankfulness to God for at least some things is an experience which every man has had at some time or other. On recovery from a serious illness, escape from accident, receiving some utterly unexpected or undeserved fortune: at such moments our hearts are spontaneously thankful, even though such gratitude may seem at first thought only very dimly related to God.

Such experience of thankfulness is often shallow and temporary, and by no means limited to those who believe in God. But Christian thankfulness is something much deeper than this. Gratitude which is distinctively Christian is not a momentary and surface experience, called forth by some spectacular event in our lives. Rather it is a stable and persistent mood of perpetual thankfulness to God, and is always rooted and grounded in a deep conviction that the whole of our life is under God's providence.

As we penetrate more and more deeply into the life of Christian praying our inner vision perceives the finger of God working in and upon our lives, and in the lives of our fellow men, not only in a few events, but in all events. Where formerly we recognized the action of God only or primarily in spectacular happenings, now we discover the hidden action of God in the most seemingly trivial occurrences and circumstances. The practice of the presence of God opens our eyes to his perpetual presence and action in all that the whole day and night bring to us. More and more of life's events, we discover, are related to God. But we have not yet reached the depths and heart of Christian thankfulness.

We remember what Paul has told us of his life for and in Christ Jesus in his letter to the Christians at Corinth:

> . . . in labours more abundant, in stripes above measure, in prisons more frequent, in deaths oft. Of the Jews five times received I forty stripes save one. Thrice was I beaten with rods, once was I stoned, thrice I suffered shipwreck, a night and a day I have been in the deep; in journeyings often, in perils of waters, in perils of robbers, in perils by mine own countrymen, in perils by the heathen, in perils in the city, in perils in the wilderness, in perils in the sea, in perils among false brethren; in weariness and painfulness, in watchings often, in hunger and thirst, in fastings often, in cold and nakedness.
> 2 Corinthians 11:23–27.

Then the words which he wrote near the close of his life, from prison in Rome to the Christians at Ephesus, take on a new significance and depth: "Giving thanks always for all things unto God and the Father in the name of our Lord Jesus Christ." Ephesians 5:20.

"Giving thanks always for all things" was no light and easy affirmation of Paul. This mood of thankfulness to God in all events, even during adversities, is one of the most dominant notes in the letters of Paul.

We need here to be most careful to give clear and accurate expression to one of the deepest of Christian convictions. What Paul gave thanks to God for was not the adversities themselves, but for the presence and action and fellowship of God in these adversities.

As we too, like Paul, give ourselves up to the creative power of Christian praying — that creative power which brings into being that which never for us existed before — we slowly find ourselves enabled truly to echo the words of this great Christian apostle:

> Who shall separate us from the love of Christ? Shall tribulation, or distress, or persecution, or famine, or nakedness, or peril, or sword? . . . Nay, in all these things we are more than conquerors through him that loved us. For I am persuaded, that neither death, nor life, nor angels, nor principalities, nor powers, nor things present, nor things to come, nor height, nor depth, nor any other creature, shall be able to separate us from the love of God, which is in Christ Jesus our Lord. Romans 8:35, 37-39.

We find ourselves, when we pray as Christians, also able to look back upon our past adversities, and to see how God never abandoned us during them. Although at the time we did not realize it, never were we separated from his presence nor from his saving love. In the adversities as in the blessings God was working slowly and secretly for our deep and rich benefit. Therefore, having become awakened to his action in and through both adversities and blessings, we now give him thanks for them both.

We do not quickly or easily reach this deep level of praying. We should, however, even from the beginning, hold ever fast before our eyes the vision of this goal. If we are faithful in filling the life of Christian praying full of adoring, self-giving, and intercession, the day will surely come when we too shall enter into such Christian thankfulness to God.

Moreover we can prepare ourselves, under God, for the coming of this deep and abiding Christian thankfulness. We do so by daily giving thanks to God for all that the day has held for us, both of blessings and of adversities. Even though at such close range to the actual occurrence we may not yet be able to discern the saving action of God, yet in the light and strength of past experiences of what God has done for us, we confidently meet each trial and vicissitude, knowing that God enters into them to bring us blessing and good, and above all else that during them he gives us his companionship.

Because of this trust and confidence, rooted in past experiences, we daily turn to God at the close of each day and offer him our thankfulness for all that the day has brought to us. Thus we link this prayer of thankfulness closely with our prayer of self-giving, in which each night we gather up all that the day has held for us and thankfully place it in the hands of our Father.

This Christian thankfulness is thus not rooted and grounded in the fact that all of the day's events have been pleasing to us or according to our own will. Rather such thankfulness is rooted in the conviction that God's providence rules over and in people through all events; and that his wisdom and love know all that we need better than we do. Even when the events of the day go counter to our own will, we turn humbly, trustfully, and thankfully to him and cry our "Not my will, but thine, be done," and repeat the prayer:

> Take me from myself, and use me
> As thou wilt,
> Where thou wilt,
> When thou wilt,
> With whom thou wilt.

Slowly over many years of faithful practice of thankfulness, we find that our faith is substantiated by life. We are given hindsight to see that God, present during every blessing and adversity, did act for us redemptively. We look back and see that even the loss of our worldly possessions was necessary and best for us spiritually. We give him thanks for the lessons which we could not have learned in any other way.

We learn to give God thanks too for the lessons derived from experiences of temptation and sinning; for the deeper understanding of ourselves, our weaknesses, our frailties, our need of God and our need for obedience to him. From his action in times of temptations and sinnings we have learned ever more deeply of our own willfullness and deep-seated selfishness, and of God's amazing and abounding love. We even over the years look back upon the deaths of our loved ones, and give God thanks for the hard lessons of detachment and attachment which have come to us through them. Then we joyfully and freely entrust and return our dear ones to his never-failing care and love; and give him our newly awakened thankfulness for the earthly years of life that he gave to our loved ones. When our dear ones, still living upon the earth, go willfully or blindly into the far countries of sin, we give God thanks that not even then does he ever abandon them. Always he accompanies them, seeking to save and redeem them and to turn them back home. Even the atheist and the sceptic can, if and when they awaken to the reality of God and accept his salvation of them, give thanks to God for his patient ways of love in dealing with them.

On first thought such praying seems utterly impossible for us. Such praying would seem even to be self-delusion and self-deception. But here we are to follow the greater and deeper wisdom and counsel of those who know so much more of God's ways than we do. As we follow their counsel and faith, we find that life substantiates their counsel as true. Like the earliest Christians, we gradually find that thankfulness becomes the abiding, steadfast mood of our whole life, able to weather all adversities and storms.

Thomas à Kempis has true wisdom to give us in these matters: —

> Be thou loving and thankful to God for the least benefit that he giveth thee, and then thou shalt be the better prepared and the more worthy to receive of him greater benefits. Think the least gift that he giveth is great; and the most despisable things take as special gifts and as great tokens of love . . . It is no little thing that is given of God, for though he send pain and sorrow we should take them gladly and thankfully, since all that he suffereth to come unto us is for our ghostly health. *Imitation of Christ:* Bk. II, Ch. x.[1]

Not only is thankfulness to be offered to God, but also to men, who are often the indirect channels through whom the gift of God has come to us. We are to distinguish clearly between the giver

[1] From *The Imitation of Christ*, Thomas à Kempis. Whitford-Klein version copyright, Harper & Brothers. Used by permission.

and the channel of giving. But as we acknowledge the channel through which God has given us the blessing, we find that our lives are wondrously knit together in what is one of the deepest and strongest of all bonds — the Church. The Church of Jesus Christ is a fellowship of persons, knit together by thankfulness to God and to each other.

Although thankfulness and adoration have much in common, yet there is an important distinction between them. Adoration is essentially disinterested praying, concerned wholly with God as he is in himself. The prayer of thankfulness has always as its background that which has been done for us by God. True Christians are always a thankful people.

PART IV

"Deliver Us"

Feed us;
Lead us;
Forgive us;
Make us to persevere.

Since we are to live as we pray, and to pray as we live, in adoration, self-giving, intercession, thankfulness, Jesus has bidden us boldly turn to our Father and give utterance to those needs which lie in the very depths of our being — needs which are involved in the triune work of hallowing the Father's name, of the coming of the Father's kingdom, and of the doing of the Father's will; the need of spiritual feeding of our lives — body, mind, spirit, will; the need of guidance and resisting power against temptation; the need of forgiveness for the sins of the world: and in and behind all of these needs there is the call from God the Father to us to persevere unto him unto our life's end.

11

Devotional Reading

ALL LIVING THINGS grow by taking in material from the outside, which they digest and assimilate; in other words, they grow by nourishment. This basic law of all biological life holds equally true for the life of prayer. Adoration, self-giving, intercession, thankfulness — all of these four kinds of praying require nourishing, if they are to grow and fulfill God's purposes for us in praying — that we shall enter into saving, intimate companionship with God. For growth in Christian praying one main source is the faithful practice of devotional reading.

Before we take up the actual practice itself, we need to understand what it is that God is seeking to do with us and for us in such reading. God's purpose precedes our practice. Never are we for a moment to forget the prevenient action of God in all that we do.

In the life of praying, we find ourselves being acted upon by One unto whom our hearts are open, every desire known, and from whom no secret can be hid. The ancient Psalmist knew this and has wondrously given expression to it in words that also become our words:

O Lord, thou hast searched me out, and known me.
Thou knowest my downsitting, and mine uprising;
Thou understandest my thoughts long before.
Thou art about my path, and about my bed;
And art acquainted with all my ways.
For lo, there is not a word in my tongue,
But thou, O Lord, knowest it altogether.

We believe by faith that God knows us through and through, and that his knowledge of us is very different from that which others have of us or which we have of ourselves. We can and do hide ourselves from others and from ourselves; but we do not and cannot hide anything from God.

We know ourselves only in a most fragmentary way. We are, and ever in this life shall remain, in many ways, mysteries to ourselves and to each other. We shall never in this life come to know all that happens to us and in us. Much of our self-knowledge leads us nowhere and is purposeless; it bears no fruit either in the form of spiritual growth or as salvation from sin.

But as we enter ever more deeply and fully into the life of Christian praying, we come to see and to know ourselves with a new kind of self-knowledge, different from that which we gain from any other source. It is a knowledge which comes to us from

God and from him alone. Spiritual insight into self which comes to us in the life of Christian praying gives us a very different knowledge of ourselves from that which we obtain from psychology, physiology, or sociology. For it is a knowledge of ourselves in relationship to God and to his redemptive purposes for our lives. It is a knowledge which convicts us of sin, because it makes us see our lives in contrast to the glory and holiness and love of God. Out of this twin knowledge — of God and of ourselves — is born the beginning of a new and deeper fellowship with God. It is a saving knowledge. In it we gain a knowledge of ourselves as a whole, as a unity, and always in relation to God. It is a knowledge which sets us free from self-centeredness and pride. It is a knowledge which humbles us and brings us peace.

We are convinced that God knows us as we truly are — something very different from what people think we are, or from what we like to pretend that we are. Until we learn that we are lost, apart from God, we cannot be saved. Our gaining of true and saving self-knowledge is the vital prerequisite of our turning to God and entreating him to save us from ourselves.

Unfortunately we are prone to resist this penetrating and humiliating gift from God. To see ourselves as we truly are in his sight is a costly, humiliating, and deflating experience. We shrink from it by many subtle and hidden self-deceptions and resistances. St. Augustine in his book *The Confessions* acutely and accurately describes to us this deep, inner resistance to true self-knowledge from God. He writes:

> But thou, O Lord, whilst he (Pontitianus) was speaking, didst turn me towards myself, taking me from behind my back, where I had placed myself while unwilling to exercise self-scrutiny; and thou didst set me face to face with myself, that I might behold how foul I was, and how crooked and sordid, bespotted and ulcerous. And I beheld and loathed myself; and whither to fly from myself I discovered not. And if I sought to turn my gaze away from myself, he continued his narrative, and thou again opposedst me unto myself and thrustedst me before my own eyes, that I might discover my iniquity, and hate it. I had known it, but acted as though I knew it not, — winked at it, and forgot it. *Confessions:* Bk. VIII, Ch. vii.[1]

Just because of our deep-seated resistance to accepting this divine gift of true self-knowledge, we require — all of us — disciplined and determined acts by which we voluntarily and joyfully seek to fulfill the necessary preconditions of receiving this knowledge concerning ourselves.

Devotional reading is one of the very greatest

[1] From *The Confessions of Saint Augustine.* Tr. by J. G. Pilkington. Liveright Publishing Corporation. Used by permission.

schools of self-knowledge. From such reading, faithfully and regularly followed over many years, we receive from God a kind of self-knowledge which is not to be had from any other source. In such reading we have interpreted to us by the great spiritual experts of the ages the mysteries of God's actions in and upon us. But unfortunately there exists widespread misunderstanding and ignorance both of the purpose and methods of this kind of reading. Devotional reading is often neglected because it is not understood. One of our deepest spiritual needs is to learn how to read devotionally, prayerfully.

Devotional reading is not at all like other kinds of reading. It is distinctive. Our usual methods of reading newspapers, magazines, and books; our methods of study: these are of little help to us in this matter. In fact they often constitute real handicaps. For devotional reading requires of us a very different mood. When we read newspapers and magazines we skim over them hurriedly. When we study, our intellects are naturally critical, argumentative, and analytical. Such reading is primarily the work of only a part of our being, — our intellects. But in devotional reading we engage not simply our intellects, but our whole being. We become quiet, receptive, expectant, docile, and above all else, humble. Any attempt on our part to ferret out the hidden mysteries of God by our own abilities will result in total failure. What cleverness and pride cannot accomplish is accomplished by humility.

Certain analogies throw revealing light upon this mood, which is so essential in devotional reading. First, there is the analogy of coming to know and appreciate a great work of art. No passing and hurried glance at a great painting as we stroll down the corridors of an art gallery will ever suffice to reveal to us its richness and significance. If we sit down in a quiet gallery and limit our attention to a single picture, then it will act upon us. For a great painting is an active agent and can affect us. We need therefore to sit receptive, open-minded, alert, quiet, before it. Furthermore, no single inspection is sufficient. Many repeated visits to the same painting are required before we begin to grasp its significance. We know that we must wait patiently until, in its own way and time, it discloses its meanings. The truth in the painting must find and fit the need that is in us. We go then to the painting in many different moods.

So, too, it is with devotional reading. We narrow down our attention to a few very great books of devotion, or even to a single book. We read them humbly, in quietude, open-minded, alert, docile, and ponder them faithfully over many years. Slowly God reveals through this reading saving truths concerning himself and concerning us.

Another helpful analogy is that of the farmer sowing his seed. The farmer places the seed in the ground, which he has prepared for it. He knows that great and mysterious powers and energies both in the seed and in the ground act — very largely without his help or direction. He knows that his part in the whole process of agriculture is an important and necessary one, but nevertheless a minor part. The great work of agriculture is not done by him, but for him. Rain, sun, air, soil, seed — all of these work together to bring about the slow and hidden processes of germination and growth. Long before any visible action occurs above the surface of the ground comes the sinking downward into the soil depths of the vital roots, upon which all later growth depends. All of this underground work is hidden from the farmer's sight and goes on "he knows not how." Only after this hidden work is accomplished does the green shoot appear above the ground and only after weeks and perhaps months will the harvest come.

Devotional reading is like farming. We plant the word-seeds in the ground of our lives, but it is God who must give the increase. We prepare the ground of heart and mind and will through living faithfully and deeply the whole life of Christian praying. Like the farmer we know that time must elapse between the planting and the harvesting.

The word-seeds must have time to sink their roots into our innermost being. The harvest of what is sown today may not come to us for many years. We know, too, like the farmer, that not all of the seed will germinate and bring any harvest. But like the farmer we have faith and hope that a goodly portion of the seed will some day bear a harvest.

We save ourselves much discouragement and sense of futility if we grasp the truth that time must elapse between the sowing and the harvest. So often we confuse the "making of a meditation" with devotional reading. They are two very different things. In meditation we engage our intellect and will upon a predetermined and self-chosen theme, usually from Holy Scriptures. We then seek to think upon the material, ending with a definite application of the passage to our own life. But this is not devotional reading. Devotional reading is more akin to "contemplation" than to "meditation." For in contemplation the work is not done by us, but to us. In contemplation we give an essentially effortless and loving attention to God and allow him to do what he wills with us. God is the active agent, and not we. God gives; we receive. Contemplation is not subject to our own command. When contemplation comes, it is given by God. So, too, in devotional reading it is God who is the revealing agent so far as the harvest is concerned. We sow; God giveth the increase.

When the harvest comes, it always bears the mark of being not our work, but God's.

We select then a few truly great devotional books and concentrate upon them. We are apt to read too many books, and then to read them only superficially and haphazardly. We can assume beyond much doubt that even in one hundred years most of the contemporary books will no longer be read, or even known. We feed our lives then upon the truly great classics of devotion, books which already have stood the test of time and circumstance. There are such devotional classics and they will be read even a thousand years from now.

Much harm and futility come from reading too many books. St. Francis de Sales, that great spiritual genius of sixteenth-seventeenth century France and Savoy, gives us the vivid analogy of bees making honey. In the late spring and early summer, when there is such an abundance and profusion of flowers, the bees do not gather the best honey, because they then flit from flower to flower and do not go deep into the honey sacs. Only later in the season, when the flowers are far less profuse, and the bees are thus compelled to go down into the depths of the honied flowers, do the bees make the finest and the sweetest honey.

So, too, it is with devotional reading. Skimming over or browsing through many religious books never gives us the deep insight and awakenings into the rich depths of the great religious works. We do our best and most fruitful devotional reading by limiting it to a few very great books, and rereading these over and over again.

Behind the devotional book we always find a saint of God, a man or a woman who is an expert in the things of the spirit. Long years of faithful obedience to the Indwelling Spirit have given them their wisdom. We turn to their books not primarily to expose our lives to ideas and thoughts, but rather to enter into holy friendship with a friend of God, and through him enter into a deeper and richer friendship with God himself.

We go to school and sit humbly at the feet of a saint of God, and catch from him by contagion his wondrous companionship with God. All of us have still very much to learn in these matters — about God, about ourselves, and about God's workings in us. We sorely need expert guides and interpreters of these great spiritual mysteries. The saints know and love God much more than we do. They speak to us of God with authority. We turn to them through their books, beseeching them to enroll us in the ranks of their disciples, promising to be both humble and docile. Rich spiritual friendships await us in God's saints through such reading.

We read and reread a book by a saint of God

for many years, and over the years find much that is new each time that we open it. But we never get the fullest insight into what the saint has to teach us of God until we enter into the creative power of the discipline of praying daily for the saint, whose book we read. We must come to know the saint if we are to know the depths of his teaching. Daily we pray:

O God, I give thee thanks for thy servant . . . Grant that I may sit humbly at his feet, and be taught through him of thee, who art his Lord and mine; that so I may be more truly thy servant to my fellow men.

Then we find that what was before hidden from our sight now becomes luminous. Praying daily for the saint bestows upon us a sensitiveness and understanding of his teaching, which we cannot get in any other way.

As we pray daily for the saint, we enter into a living friendship with him through the veil, giving ourselves deeply and joyously to this friendship. We find ourselves looking forward eagerly to the time when we shall meet him face to face in the kingdom that lies beyond death, and can thank him for all that he has taught us of God.

Spiritual growth comes from reading devotional books slowly and meaningfully. The rush and speed of modern life does not make it easy for us to go at the pace of "not faster than a walk." Rushing through a book of devotion never gives us its rich harvest. Much is to be gained by the practice of reading these books word by word, lingering and pondering over individual words and their meaning. So many of our common English words have depths and imagery to which we are dulled and insensitive unless we give them our complete and detached interest. As a word or phrase in a devotional book seizes our attention, and a thought comes to us, we at once stop reading and give our full attention to the thought, as coming to us in the providence of God. We let its power take full possession of us and lead us where it will.

We underline the words which have caught our attention. Marginal notes made as we read can serve to point out to us in future rereadings the thoughts which came to us previously, and enable us again to think upon them. Each time that we reread a devotional book we mark passages to which we were blind before. This is evidence that we have grown spiritually. One good devotional book, read and reread over decades, becomes a book which is well marked. At each reading we are a different person, and therefore words which meant nothing to us in previous readings now strike our attention. Let us always thank God for this increased spiritual insight. The blank pages at the end of the book can well be used to form our own index, so that in times of spiritual need we can quickly turn to special passages which are of help.

In any single reading we find only a few words which become luminous for us. Getting spiritual help is a progressive growth, even though slow. We are to be patient, remembering the analogy of the farmer planting his seed. We are to be content to plant the word-seeds and then to wait over years for the sure harvest. The great classics of devotion are to become life-companions, not simply books to be read once and then placed aside upon a bookshelf, never to be looked at or thought of again.

Gradually we form the practice of never ending the day's devotional reading without a spontaneous act of giving thanks to God for the insights which have come to us. These little acts of thankfulness are important, for they serve to build up in us the mood of thankfulness to God, and this prepares us to receive further insight in the future. For the insights that come to us in devotional reading are the gifts of God; they are not the accomplishments of our own prowess. To give God thanks for them is to deepen and strengthen in us the conviction that they have come to us from God as gifts. Often we receive no fuller insights because we have not taken the time to offer thanks to God for the insights we have already received;

or because we have not entered upon such reading humbly, prayerfully, receptively.

Still a further factor in this kind of reading is that we should always seek to apply the truths we perceive to ourselves, rather than to the lives of others. It is usually more pleasant to apply uncomfortable truths to the lives of others than to ourselves. Where suggestions come spontaneously to our minds, and where we are convinced they come to us from God and not from our own desiring, then we may apply the truths perceived to the lives of others. Generally speaking, we do well to remember that any light thrown upon the lives of others may very profitably also be applied to ourselves.

What particular books are best suited as devotional reading to nourish our praying? First and foremost always comes the Bible, especially the New Testament. We notice in all other books of devotional reading how deeply saturated they are in reference to the Gospel accounts of Jesus' words and deeds. Like them, we too are to saturate our minds and hearts with the words of the Gospels. Take one of the four Gospels, and for a whole year read and reread it over and over again, always slowly, always lovingly, always prayerfully, always humbly. There is much more spiritual food in any one of the Gospels than a whole lifetime can exhaust. Go to school and sit humbly at the feet of Mark, or Luke, or Matthew, or John. Pray daily for him, that through his words God may teach you something of the limitless mystery of his Christ, that you may become a more faithful interpreter of his life to your fellow men. In a second year turn to another Gospel record, or perhaps to the book of the Acts. Another year go to school at the feet of Paul, or of John, in their letters.

On some days we may read only a few words or sentences. Another day we read a whole chapter or several pages. The reading cannot be measured by any rigid pattern. We are rather to follow the dim guidance of the Indwelling Spirit. When we consider Jesus' own life, we note that in every crisis the words of Scripture from his lips give expression to his own experiences, to be the light and strength to him in temptation. When we examine the lives of the saints, we find in their writings also deep insights into the Bible, which rebuke our own meager familiarity with it.

Outside of the scriptural material there exist many well-tested devotional classics, any one of which might well become our teacher for life. But none of these is ever to be permitted to become the substitute for the Scriptures themselves. We must count it a serious sin when we yield to the temptation to turn only to such books rather than to the Bible.

Many of us have found over years of devotional reading that one of the very greatest of the classics of devotion is *The Imitation of Christ*. Some of us would rank it second only to the Holy Scriptures themselves as devotional material. But we are not to let ourselves become immersed in the fruitless discussion of whether Thomas à Kempis or Gerard Groote was the author. What we need to do is to read and heed the great spiritual wisdom which the book contains. The book can offer us a rare spiritual companionship with a man who knew both God and man intimately and accurately. There is hardly a page in the book which does not arrest our attention, and which does not have power to teach us much about God and about ourselves, leading us into ever deeper and more intimate friendship with God.

More and more of us are finding another rare spiritual companionship in François de Fénelon, the great and saintly Archbishop of Cambrai in the late seventeenth century. Those of us who have fed long and deeply upon his writings, whether in the original French or in English translations, know that we have been taught by one who was a master in spiritual matters. François de Fénelon knows very deeply and accurately about the distinctively Christian life of praying; about God's amazing love for us sinners; about the nature of distinctively Christian love from man to God. His deep teachings issued from a life of much suffering, and he himself lived all that he taught to others. We shall acquire much spiritual wisdom if we turn to him as our spiritual guide and friend.

Another truly great classic of devotion is *The Confessions of St. Augustine,* written in northern Africa at the close of the fourth century. St. Augustine has rich and penetrating knowledge to give us about the prevenience and grace of God and our terrible resistances to him. He is a spiritual friend who grows upon us more and more as we read and reread his book.

All of us will surely come to love Nicholas Herman (or, as he is more commonly known, Brother Lawrence), the humble layman who worked in the kitchen of a Carmelite monastery in Paris in the seventeenth century. His book is only a very small one, but he has much to teach us about practicing the presence of God. His simple and dominant conviction of the immediate, loving presence of God is such a contagious one that imperceptibly we find ourselves copying his practice, and learning to find God present in all the tedium and routine of our day's work. His little book is entitled *The Practice of the Presence of God.*

Thomas Kelly's *A Testament of Devotion* offers us great spiritual help, marked by such simplicity and humility that every one of us who reads this book learns much from its author.

A short bibliography of good devotional books is given at the end of this chapter. Purchase some or all of them, and then settle down for years, if not your whole lifetime, of reading and rereading them.

The most immediate task of all in connection with devotional reading is the forming of a disciplined habit of reading. Our lives are already too full of too many things. To add a period of time daily for devotional reading seems at first thought to be asking for the impossible. How can we find time to do such reading? How can we be assured that it will be done regularly, day after day? There are times when we have a real inclination and desire to do such reading. But we also know that on many days we have no pressing desire or even inclination to do it. Such reading cannot be left to mood, to need, to inclination. Let us root our reading of devotional books in God's will, not in our own fluctuating moods. Because we want to live for God, for his glory, and to fulfill God's will that we enter into intimate fellowship with him; and because we want our fellow men also to enter into that holy fellowship with God: therefore we lovingly and obediently enter upon the discipline which will ensure that we do this devotional reading daily. If such reading is to fulfill God's purpose for it, it must be done as regularly as we take in our physical food.

We always find time for the things we count important and want to do. Daily we find time to hear and read the words of the world. Most of us have little difficulty in finding time to read a morning or evening newspaper. We also find time to listen to at least one radio program each day. We deem it important to hear and to heed the words of the world. Seldom do we allow anything to prevent our doing this. We can link our loving discipline of devotional reading with these strongly established habits of attending to the words of the world.

Therefore we lovingly and willingly and obediently enter upon the discipline of not reading the newspapers, or turning on the radio, until we have completed our devotional reading for the day. Unless we have the help and motivation of some such discipline, we do not get this devotional reading done. Either it gets postponed to some later hour — and then the day has a way of getting so full of many things that it does not get done at all — or it will be done only intermittently. All of us need to clear a definite, regular time each day for this reading of the words of God. It should be a time free from ordinary interruptions. Even ten minutes each morning on the train would soon form a firm habit of devotional reading. Even ten minutes after the children go off to school, and before the household chores are started, will, over the years, bear much fruit. Our lack of any regular and disciplined practice of devotional reading constitutes a serious judgment upon our spiritual life. Once we undertake to do this reading, we soon find that we want to do it and look forward eagerly to doing it, for it leads us into an ever deeper friendship with God. When because of conditions beyond our control we sometimes have to omit it, we feel a real lack and hunger. Over the years we find that this reading brings to our lives through the spiritual friendships of the saints a wondrous companionship with God.

Books for Devotional Reading

1. François de Fénelon (1651–1715)
   Christian Perfection. Harper & Brothers, 1947.
   Spiritual Letters. Idlewild Press, 1945.

2. Thomas à Kempis (1380–1471)
   The Imitation of Christ.
   Harper & Brothers, Whitford-Klein Edition.
   E. P. Dutton & Co., Inc., Everyman's Library Edition.

3. Brother Lawrence (1611–1691)
   The Practice of the Presence of God.
   The Judson Press.
   Benziger Brothers, Inc.

4. Saint Francis of Assisi (1182–1226)
   Little Flowers of Saint Francis. E. P. Dutton & Co., Inc.
   Brother John, by Vida Scudder. E. P. Dutton & Co., Inc.
   Little Plays of St. Francis, by Lawrence Housman. Sidgwick and Jackson, Ltd. (England).

5. Saint Augustine (354-430)
    The Confessions.
        E. P. Dutton & Co., Inc., Everyman's Library Edition.
        Liveright Publishing Corp.

6. Thomas Kelly
    A Testament of Devotion. Harper & Brothers.

7. W. L. Sperry
    Strangers and Pilgrims. Little, Brown & Company.

12

Temptation and Praying

WHEN WE LIVE deeply and fully the life of Christian praying — in adoration, self-giving, intercession, and thankfulness — new and saving insights come to us from God. In devotional reading we gain much help and guidance for the whole of our living. We gain deep and saving knowledge in dealing with that inner warfare of the soul which we call temptation.

How desperately we need — all of us — help and wisdom and spiritual power from God in dealing with the temptations that assault our lives here upon earth. How often we wish that the Church — and especially the clergy — would give us counsel which would enable us to become victors in this inner warfare. But there are no easy short cuts to victory in these matters. Only as we live deeply and fully the whole life of Christian praying can we become truly victors — joyful victors over temptation. For Christian praying alone can bring us the power and will by which we can become victorious.

In Christian praying we turn to Christ that he may teach us how to be victorious in temptation. His is the one life which has been perfectly and fully victorious, and it is the Father's will that we shall learn our lessons in victory over temptation from him. He learned from his Father how to deal with temptation victoriously. We, too, must learn through Christ from the Father, if we are to be victors. Until we learn from God through Christ the secret of victory in this warfare, we cannot speak to others with that authority which saves.

Through Christ's encounters with temptation we are given by God the saving insight and wisdom which we need and want. We have seen that one of the basic foundations for Christian praying is that we turn to him who is the untempted and the sinless. In him and in no other we find the secret of victory. The Father's gift of saving wisdom comes to us through his Christ, who like us met all temptations common to man, but unlike us was without sin. In his life consent to temptation was never given. "Lord, teach us the secret of victory, which thou didst learn from thy Father."

Jesus' life was one which was ever turned to his Father in deepest, truest adoration, self-giving, intercession, and thankfulness. He ever sought to know and to do his Father's will. To that will his whole life was unbrokenly and perpetually dedicated, gladly given in holy obedience. In Jesus we behold a life at all points truly human, yet devoted with complete and perfect self-giving to the hallowing of his Father's name, to the coming of his Father's kingdom, and to the unswerving doing of his Father's will. In Jesus we are given by God a life seeking nothing for himself, but ever living for others, offering himself wholly and perfectly to his Father "for their sakes." His was the one, true, pure, and perfect interceding life, because he was wholly set free from all service of himself. Also his was a life dominated from beginning to end by thankfulness, able even in the heart of adversity to turn to his Father and cry, "Father, I thank thee." His life was deeply saturated with the words of God to his people. He had pondered long and deeply and lovingly upon the Holy Scriptures, and in them he found a knowledge of his Father's will.

In Jesus we see vividly and unforgettably a life which, just because it was given whole-heartedly and unswervingly to adoration, self-giving, intercession, and thankfulness, was always victorious over every temptation.

Jesus feared his Father. For true fear of God is in no way incompatible with true love for God. The fear which Christian love casts out is fear of the world. Jesus himself enjoined his disciples to fear God as he feared God. Jesus knew the saving power of godly fear. His was a fear not for himself, of what might happen to him. But his was a fear lest God's name be profaned, God's kingdom not come, and the Father's will be not done — and therefore men perish. Such a fear, wholly free from self-regard, and concerned only for God's glory and man's salvation, is holy fear. Unless he continued steadfast and unswerving in faithfulness and obedience to his Father, men would be lost forever. The glory of God and the salvation of men were the powerful motivations for his utter obedience, an obedience which led him, rather than swerve one step from the will of his Father, to the cross.

We, too, like Jesus, can be victors over temptation only in so far as we live fully the life of Christian praying. When we adore, give, intercede, and are thankful; and when we nourish these kinds of praying with regular and loving devotional reading — then we too shall receive into our lives the wisdom, power, and will to obey God, when we are confronted with the conflict between our will and God's will. Unless we have holy fear of God, which will lead us to obedience to him, we fail God and because of our disobedience and faithlessness others perish.

In every temptation the issue is ultimately to be traced back to variants of but one thing, — the conflict between our will and God's will. Instead of looking toward God, we are seeking self-gain or our own pleasure. We are being tempted to turn away from God-centeredness to self-centeredness. We are taking back from God our total and unconditional self-giving. We are seeking to rest from continued and deeper self-giving to God. We are shutting our eyes to the needs of our fellow men and thus refusing to participate in the life of intercession. Instead of living for them, we are seeking to live for ourselves. We are silencing and ignoring the echo of those words of God which we have stored in our inner life in devotional reading. Which shall we obey — self or God? That is the ultimate issue of every temptation. Whose will is to be done — ours or God's?

What we face in temptation is no rational and academic choice. In the moments of actual temptation there is no time to sit down coolly and evaluate and decide on intellectual grounds. The assault of temptation is savage. We cannot see the issues in cold and disinterested fashion. The issue hangs upon a thread. One step yielded, one moment of delay and faltering, and we are swept away as by a mighty current. What we must rely upon in the actual moment of temptation is not reason, but the whole power of prayer, built up over the years. If we have been faithful to God in our life of praying, we know spontaneously what to do, and we do it with loving obedience.

For years we have been practicing adoration —

the disinterested, unselfish turning to God. We have founded the discipline, so sorely needed now in the time of temptation, of turning at once to God and giving ourselves trustfully and unconditionally to him in holy obedience. Our life has been saturated with intercession — that life in which we live for others, forgetting ourselves. Now in our moments of temptation we unpremeditatingly know that "for their sakes" we dare not fail God or them.

Even thankfulness will have its part to play also, as we are soon to see. There will come to us a rich harvest from the hours of faithful sowing of the words of God in our lives in times of devotional reading. We shall understand the truth and wisdom of Thomas à Kempis:

> Write my words in thy heart diligently, and oft think thou upon them; for in time of temptation they shall be much necessary unto thee. That which thou understandest not when thou readest it, thou shalt understand in the time of my visitation. *Imitation of Christ:* Bk. III, Ch. iii.[1]

As we look back over the years of temptation, from the perspective of Christian praying, we realize as we never have before important truths concerning these temptations. Whereas without

[1] From *The Imitation of Christ*, Thomas à Kempis. Whitford-Klein version copyright, Harper & Brothers. Used by permission.

serious praying we often did not even know that we were being tempted, now within the life of Christian praying we have become more sensitive to the myriad and seemingly trivial forms which temptation takes. Matters which formerly seemed quite irrelevant to God now take on a grave importance. For this greater and truer sensitiveness to the God-given warnings of oncoming evil, we give unceasing thanks to God.

From our praying we gain a new insight into the nature of awareness of God's warnings in our temptations. The very awareness of temptation requires adequate interpretation and explanation. From the vantage point of Christian praying we waken to the fact that the awareness of temptation is itself the gift of God to us. It is something given to us and not simply of our own making. We are made aware of temptation by the action of the prevenient God. No evil can attack our lives without the full knowledge and immediate action of God. As soon as evil strikes at us, God gives us warning by making us aware of temptation. Is this not at least something of the unusual counsel of St. James in his Epistle: ". . . count it all *joy* when ye fall into divers temptations"?

This joy is spiritual and something very different from superficial and temporary pleasure. It is rather the deep-seated and abiding mood of peace and trust in God, that he will deliver us from all

TEMPTATION AND PRAYING 175

evil. Over the years as we pray we learn to turn to God immediately when temptation strikes at our life, and to thank God for the gift of awareness, of warning. This thankfulness is a mighty source of strength and obedience.

In our temptations we are given by God a deeper knowledge of ourselves, a knowledge very different from that self-knowledge which we gain from any other source. This God-given self-knowledge is a spiritual knowledge of ourselves. Gradually in our praying we learn to desire and to expect God's testings, knowing that this testing is necessary for each of us. God, we remember, knows us through and through. But we are not ever to presume to lead ourselves into temptations, seeking to test ourselves. Only in the temptations that come involuntarily to us, permitted by God, do we gain saving self-knowledge. For only in the temptations that come to us under his providence may we find the grace to enable us to encounter them victoriously. When we lead ourselves into temptation, we then encounter them without the sustaining, conquering grace of God.

We gain great strength when we remember that no temptation can come to us without God's full knowing and caring. Long before we awaken to the fact of temptation, God knows and warns us. God does not wait until we ask him for saving grace. From him comes first of all the warning, given to us in our awareness of temptation. Here we see clearly the relevance of the doctrine of prevenience to our praying. God always warns us of each coming danger. Often we do not heed his warnings that what we face is evil. Often we defy and rebel against this warning. But then it ceases to be temptation and becomes sin. God, and not we, is the ever alert watchman over our lives. Thus in the Garden of Gethsemane it is Jesus who in the midst of his agony watches prayerfully and lovingly over the three sleeping disciples, and not they who keep watch over him.

Because of this deep conviction of God's full concern for us in every moment of temptation, we know that we are never left alone to meet it. Always at our side is our Saviour and our God. We have only to turn immediately to him, to keep steadfastly trusting in him, and the tempting thought cannot defeat us. All that God sees and knows that we need, he at once offers to us, if we are humble enough to accept it. Never can we claim that we had to yield to temptation. Every yielding to temptation is sin, and no power can make us yield until we give our consent to the temptation and let it enter our inner life. Evil can only knock at the outside of our inner life; it cannot enter until we open the door to it. It can knock; it can annoy us; it can be importunate: but it cannot enter until we give our consent and open our interior life to it. To let evil come inside is sin.

We need carefully to distinguish between temptation and sin. We have the strengthening consolation of knowing that Christ was tempted. So long as temptation comes to us unsought, and so long as something within us resists — however small that something is — we are not to lose heart. We are to rejoice that under the guidance of the Indwelling Spirit something in us resists the temptation of evil. For the glory of God, and for the sake of the salvation of our fellow men, we obey the warning and the counsel of the voice of the Indwelling Spirit.

As we reflect upon past temptations we come to realize that often the siege of temptation either preceded or followed work which God meant us to do. Although we did not realize at the time the particular purpose that evil had in tempting us, now, looking backward upon that which followed, we can see that evil struck at our lives in order to divert us or disqualify us from doing the work of God for his children. Looking back now, we can see that if we had yielded to temptation then, we would not have been able to help the person whom God was bringing to us that he might through us find help and light from God. So often does God send to us his needy children, that we must be strong in resisting temptation, so that when they come to us in the providence of God we may not fail them. The awareness that faithfulness in resisting temptation concerns not only ourselves but others constitutes a strong incentive to loving obedience to God in every temptation. "For their sakes" we will persevere in resisting every temptation.

Temptation also follows times of spiritual exaltation. We have just gone through moments of spiritual insight and joy. Perhaps we have just been awakened through repentance to the gift of God's free forgiveness; or we have had a new and deeper experience of dedication of our lives to God. After such experiences we believe that we can never again fail God. But, as we look back upon these times of exaltation, we know that inevitably they were followed by times of doubt and temptation. We doubted the validity of the experience we had just gone through. Was it only a delusion after all? Our surest and wisest procedure in such times is never to make any decision, important or incidental, except in the mood of prayer. The convictions which came to us in moments of spiritual exaltation were born out of the quiet realization of the presence of God. Therefore they can only wisely and truly be judged from within the mood of devotion. The moods of temptation, scepticism, or fear are never the proper moods for making spiritual decisions. In every doubt and uncertainty we turn to God in adoration, self-giving, intercession, and thankfulness; we turn again to the wisdom contained in books of devotion, and wait patiently and peacefully for God's saving word.

Only if we live truly, deeply, and faithfully in the whole life of Christian praying can we become victorious over temptation. There are no easy short cuts to victory. The life of Christian praying brings us spiritual joy and the peace of God which passes all human understanding. By ourselves, imprisoned in self-centeredness, we fail, we yield, and we sin. But when our lives are centered in God, we have the victory. Our will — or God's will? Temptation is our testing.

13

Sin, Forgiveness and Praying

AFTER WE BUILD our Christian praying upon the foundations of Christian convictions, we find that we possess new and saving insights in dealing with the power of sin. In life we have to deal not only with temptations, but also with sin — the temptations which we have yielded to, given our consent to, and which now live on in us with their mighty power, blinding us, paralyzing our will, goading us into further sin, enslaving us. The life of Christian praying has much saving wisdom to give to us for dealing victoriously with sin, for in praying we enter into the mighty wonder of God's loving dealing with us as sinners, and awaken to the cost which God pays for our sins.

The heart of all sin is selfishness — the will to do our own will and to refuse to do God's will. Confronted with the choice between God's will and our own, the choosing of our will is sin. Sin is our "No" to God's offer to us of theocentric life, with all of its joy and peace and power. The heart of the problem of sin is not the sinful deeds, but rather the source of those deeds — the self-willed and self-centered "I." It does little good to check and stop the external sinful acts, if the sinful self is left in its self-centeredness. The problem is to win by love the sinful self, so that it will turn to God in humble and full surrender of itself, so that it will say with saving faith, "Not my will, but Thine be done."

Deep and saving truths, which the redeeming God and the indwelling God give to us, come to us only slowly over the years. We have to awaken to the sham and deceit of our human kind of freedom, before we are ready to experience the true freedom which is ours when we enter freely and lovingly into that servitude to God which is also sonship. After years of praying as Christians — for it comes to us only slowly — we look back over our own spiritual history and give God unutterable and unceasing thanks for his wondrous and unwearied patience and courtesy in dealing with us as sinners. Looking backward, we can begin to understand something of the mighty wisdom of God, which allowed us to go through those many years in which we sought to deal with our sinfulness by our own wisdom and will power. We see now that it was his patient love which allowed us to be defeated over and over again, as we sought to rule and govern our own lives, apart from him. We rejoice in the divine strategy of salvation.

We give God our deep and abiding thankfulness that step by step he has led us and pushed us into the experience of our own spiritual bankruptcy. He teaches us that until we root our whole life in truly Christian praying, building such praying upon stalwart Christian faith in God, we cannot enter into any life which will bring us true joy and peace. We smile now at ourselves, as we look back and remember the many excuses we offered in our failures. We thought then that all that we needed was more knowledge. More knowledge was given us, and still we found that we were not freed from sinning. At times, with the sting of recent defeat disturbing our minds, we were able to watch and refrain from sinning. But always, when least we expected it, and from some unguarded flank, the powers of evil again struck at our lives; we gave our consent, and again we sinned. We learned in our hearts the undebatable truth of the old words, which Paul wrote:

For to will is present with me; but how to perform that which is good I find not. For the good that I would, I do not; but the evil which I would not, that I do. Romans 7:18.

We remember now, as we look back over the years from the vantage point of Christian praying, the many excuses and self-deceptions we offered to ourselves and to others. We offered them to ourselves because we did not dare to offer them to God. We offered them to others because we knew that their judgment was an easy one, and very different from God's. We looked about us and found that all other men were in the same predicament as ourselves. We solaced ourselves with the thought that where all fail, victory is therefore impossible. We drove from our memories the stubborn fact of the sinless Christ — God's true man. We told ourselves that the victorious life was only an "ideal." We also remember looking about us and being able to find others much worse than we were. At least we were not as they.

We tried repeatedly to believe these self-deceptions; but the indwelling God would not let us find any peace in this refuge of self-deception. We dared not read the Bible or a devotional classic, lest we be confronted with the voice which would speak through the words of the book, "Thou art the man." The voice which not all our sinning can ever silence whispered to our souls in unguarded moments that all our excuses were lies. We dared not face God; and we dared not face ourselves. Later in this book we shall see that this fear of facing God and self operates to keep men from attending a "retreat" and thus entering into that silence in which we are left utterly alone in the presence of God. Instead of facing God or ourselves, we tried to busy ourselves with a multitude of external activities, so that we should have no time to hear that voice. We stopped going to church, lest there we might hear the convicting Word of God speaking to us in the words of a prayer, a hymn, a sermon. We stopped reading the Bible. We put it away upon a shelf, where we would not even have to see it. Instead we read the newspapers and novels. We were determined not to hear God's Word. We willed not to repent. But the Indwelling Spirit pricked us with unrest and fear and boredom. We feared the world, and the truth concerning ourselves. We feared God, not with holy love, but with slavish fear, which never saves.

For it is none other than God the Redeemer and God the Indwelling Spirit who slowly leads us and presses us into despair. We flee God down through the days and years of our lives, but no matter where we may flee to, on arriving we find God already there. Francis Thompson has given expression to this experience in *The Hound of Heaven*.

I fled Him, down the nights and down the days;
  I fled Him, down the arches of the years;
I fled Him, down the labyrinthine ways
  Of my own mind; and in the mist of tears
I hid from Him, and under running laughter.
      Up vistaed hopes, I sped;
      And shot, precipitated,
Adown Titanic glooms of chasmèd fears,
  From those strong Feet that followed, followed after.

> But with unhurrying chase,
> And unperturbèd pace,
> Deliberate speed, majestic instancy,
> They beat — and a Voice beat
> More instant than the Feet —
> "All things betray thee, who betrayest Me."[1]

Finally we know that we have reached the end. We cannot take even one more step. We do not reach despair so long as we can take one more step, however little that step may be. Self-despair is our end. But it is not the end for God. For God it is in a significant sense a new beginning, the moment of entrance into the new life in which God is the center. Our self-despair is transformed into surrender to God, and acceptance of repentance as his gift. We accept self-despair and find paradoxically that it brings us peace and light. Then we awaken to the truth that God has been seeking us not for the end of condemning us, but to save and redeem us from the self-centered life which is hell.

That which we awaken to in the experience of accepted judgment from God is both repentance and forgiveness. Only Christian praying can make us aware of the depths and richness and wonder of this experience. Only when we accept God's truth concerning us — his loving, redeeming judgment

---

[1] From *The Hound of Heaven*, by Francis Thompson. Dodd, Mead & Company, Inc. Used by permission.

— do we awaken to the forgiveness of God which has prevened us. Repentance is our awakening to the forgiveness of God which was given to us immediately upon our sinning, but which we were too blinded to accept. How could we then see or know that his hands were stretched out to us, offering his sheer and free forgiveness? We could not even imagine him doing that. God did not leave us to ourselves. In the foundations which we laid for our Christian praying we saw that the New Testament doctrine of the holiness of God tells us of a Holy God who when we sin immediately takes the initiative and comes to press his holiness close to our sinfulness. It is such a stupendous thought that we cannot believe it. It is the heart of the gospel.

But in Christian praying we find what we cannot learn in any other way, that from the moment we sinned, God came to us, seeking to lead us into that repentance which would waken us to his free forgiveness. We repented because God found us, having led us into self-despair. His forgiveness did not wait until we made ourselves repentant, but has been working in and upon us all of the time, although we knew it not. We do not realize God's forgiveness until we have become repentant. Always we are to remember that the doctrine of the divine prevenience stands for the fact that much of God's work comes before we waken to it. Left to ourselves in our self-centeredness — blind and impotent — we could never have become repentant. It is the love and goodness of God which lead us into repentance.

Even when we awaken to God's free and full forgiveness we cannot believe it. Forgiveness is such an utterly unbelievable act. How can God forgive us sinners? We know not how; we only know that he does. His redeeming love staggers and shatters all of our human wisdom, all of our expectations and deserts. God has not dealt with us according to our wickedness. We thought we had to earn forgiveness. We do not like to live upon the divine charity. It is a mighty humiliation to receive God's forgiveness but it is also a humiliation which brings us perfect freedom and joy. To accept freely and humbly God's forgiveness is to escape from the misery of a self-centered life and to enter into the wondrous fellowship of man and God.

There is an amazing paradox about God's forgiveness. We know that we are forgiven by him, yet this is so utterly inconceivable and unbelievable that we still cry out — "Forgive me." It is not a momentary cry, but a cry which is ever repeated all the days of our life. For forgiveness does not bring forgetfulness to us. Always we carry about in our memories the truth that we have sinned. Sin has eternal consequences; and not the least of these is memory. Memory is God's penance for us, a penance which goes much deeper than any penance which man can assign. "Forgive me." But it is not so much the cry of the unforgiven, as the cry of him who has received and known God's forgiveness. The abiding memory of sin is no longer an undesired memory, a restless, torturing memory. We now accept it joyfully as part of the truth of what we are. In the kingdom of heaven we are not ashamed to be of the community of the forgiven. We accept humbly and willingly and peacefully the memory of past sin, and thank God for his amazing forgiveness. Forgiveness is not so much an isolated event or act, as a state into which we enter as we grow into that new life with God, which is eternal life.

As with temptations, so too with our sins, the life of true Christian adoration, self-giving, intercession, thankfulness brings us saving insights into the mighty and loving power of God's forgiveness. We give ourselves unresistingly and humbly to the Redeemer God, and live in that new life of holy obedience which takes us into that peace of God which passeth all human understanding. Thanks be to God for his saving of us both from and out of sin to free forgiveness.

The life of praying, however, must be given time to work its action in our lives. The life of Christian praying is no short-time work, quickly finished. It is a life-long labor of love for God and for man.

14

Perseverance

THE LIFE OF Christian praying is a life-long work of love, — love for God and Christian love for our fellow men. Praying is no momentary remedy for our spiritual ills and needs. Only as we learn to persevere through thick and thin and down to the end will we reap the rich harvest of Christian prayer. When we remember that we are made for God, for his glory, and for intimate fellowship with him, when we want this to be fulfilled not only in our own life but also in the lives of our fellow men, then we willingly accept the call from God to make our praying the work of a whole lifetime. When we persevere in the life of praying we soon find ourselves confronted with mighty powers of evil working upon us from without, and in us from within, seeking to divert our attention from God. One of the purposes of the life of Christian praying is to enable us to deal with these evil powers resolutely and wisely.

The powers of evil seek to divert us from God by sending us distractions. Thoughts and desires have a way of seizing our imagination and attention, and before we know it our interest is upon other matters than God. We find our lips repeating the familiar words of prayer, but our minds and hearts are intent upon other concerns. Our first thought is that such distracted praying is worthless, insincere, and wrong.

Is wandering attention something which is peculiar to praying and worshiping? Do we not find it also true in many other phases of our life? When we read a book do not our minds often wander? When we listen to a symphonic concert, do we not again and again find that our attention is distracted from the music? In the midst of carrying on conversation with others, do we not often find ourselves inattentive to what is being said? Distractions are not something peculiar to religion. They operate in many aspects of our life. How then shall we deal with them when they come to us in our praying?

If we live truly and deeply the full life of Christian praying, we know spontaneously what to do. We simply turn to God, and in turning to him, the distracting thought vanishes, we know not how. The life of adoration has built up in us the oft-repeated, and almost constant, practice of turning to God as each new event of the day comes. When distractions come, we simply turn again to God as an adorer. Looking at God, we simply drop the distraction. All distractions are self-centered, for in them we revolve about ourselves. But our praying as self-giving has taught us to give ourselves wholly and unconditionally to God repeatedly during the day, and so to become God-centered. As our attention wanders, we turn back to God and give ourselves again to him. When distractions come to us, we turn quietly and patiently to God, and catch again from him something of his uninterrupted concern for others, and we find ourselves turning from our distractions to the work of intercession. Praying as thankfulness also aids us in times of distraction. We turn to God and offer him our thanks that in and through the distractions, though we forget him, he never forgets us, and that our awareness of the distraction was his calling us back to himself.

When we learn the spiritual wisdom given in the life of praying we no longer attempt to fight the distraction. That only constitutes still another distraction. Nor do we any longer try to unravel the distracting thought, seeking to find just how and when we were diverted. Nor do we follow it, curious to see where it may take us. Instead, we immediately and effortlessly turn again to God, and the distraction vanishes. The attack of evil has failed.

We are not to be disturbed or disheartened by the persistence and frequency of the attacks. Rather we are to turn again and again to God, dropping each distraction as it comes to us in praying. We are to persevere in this. As often as they come to us, so often do we turn back to God. We do not give our conscious consent to the distractions. We want to give our whole attention to God.

Another obstacle which we face when we pray is the desire and expectation of quick and immediate results from our prayer. It is a difficulty to which we are especially open in the first stages of praying. The cure for impatience is to turn our thoughts upon the infinite, unwearied patience of God, working in both physical creation and in man. Let us keep constantly and clearly before our minds the objective of Christian praying,— the leading of us into life which is centered in God, lived for his glory and for intimate fellowship with him. That goal involves the long process of slow, gradual remaking of the old self-centered life into the new life, which is wholly God-centered. That work requires time, much time. It is a life-long work, not temporary labor. Those who deal with children know how slowly, and with how great difficulty, the child's character is shaped. How much more difficult and slow must of necessity be the work of our transformation into the life which we name eternal life. We are to approach our praying as the trained mountaineer goes at the mountain trail, with slow, short, persistent steps. The novice who rushes at the mountain trail soon finds himself breathless and exhausted. The fruits of praying are given to us by God so imperceptibly that often we do not detect them. We are to be content to pursue our praying at God's pace for us, and never to seek to anticipate God's providence.

Usually we start the life of prayer impelled by some deep and pressing need. The first days and weeks go well; we have a zest and joy in praying. We have a strong sense of its being worth while. Although we fail to recognize it, our praying is self-centered — it is for our own self-satisfaction and self-enjoyment. Then God himself, for our sakes, has to withdraw this enjoyment in order to wean us away from all self-seeking. Will we continue to pray if God does not give us enjoyment in our praying? Faced with dryness, darkness, lack of desire, monotony, will we persevere in praying, or give up? In times when prayer seems lifeless and unreal and unrewarding, we shall be tempted to abandon it. All temptation is being confronted with a choice, the choice of doing our own will, seeking our own gain; or doing the will of God. Every wrong choice — choosing our own will — means sin, deeper enslavement in the misery of self-centeredness. Every right choice — choosing to do God's will — leads us into a deeper and truer freedom. The prevenient God is acting; we **must respond.**

These times of darkness, of dryness, of unreality and monotony come to us from God, who is seeking in his wisdom to give us a deeper self-knowledge and to wean us from self-centeredness into God-centeredness, in preparation for eternal life. In such times we are to persevere in praying. When God sees that we need and can profit from gifts of sweetness and joy in praying, he will give them to us. When he withholds them, we know that he does so for our own sake. Do we pray for the gifts we get from God, or do we pray for God?

All Christian praying is intended for God, and for his glory. Christian praying can no more be rooted and grounded in feelings or emotions than it can be in the intellect. These all are only in small part subject to our control. They come and they go. Christian praying is founded upon the strong and firm foundations of the initiative of God, and the creative, redemptive, indwelling action of God in and upon us; on God's mighty sinlessness; his perfect freedom; his amazing, conquering love. If our praying is rooted in these foundations we shall not pay too much attention to our feelings in times of prayer. We pray because of God and not because of our feelings. We root our praying not in our own psychological states, but in the reality of God.

When we enter fully and truly into the life of Christian praying we do not yield to the Satanic suggestion that we pray only when we feel like it.

The fruit of prayer is not that we get what we want or ask for, but that we receive what God wills to give us and do in us. If pleasant feelings come to us in praying, we thankfully accept them, but we do not depend upon them. When God withholds them we continue to pray, for our praying is rooted in God.

Another difficulty which confronts us again and again in praying is the temptation to postpone praying — just for today. There are so many good excuses why we should not pray today. We are physically and mentally tired out and exhausted. We were up very late last night and what we really need is more sleep. It will not make any difference if just for today we omit our praying. Disciplines which may have taken years to form can very quickly be broken. We are to consider suggestions to postpone or to omit praying as being Satanic in origin, or as being the subtle seeking to escape from living under God's sovereignty and returning to self-rule and self-will, which is sin; and the only way of dealing with sin is to turn to God. In times when God's providence makes the observance of our regular disciplines impossible, we are not to hesitate for a moment to omit our regular praying. But where we are convinced that we could pray, but are selfishly seeking to escape from praying, we are to realize that yielding to this temptation is sin.

Satan knows that it is only in the present moment that we can meet God. In no way does Satan trouble himself about our intentions to meet God later in the day, or tomorrow. So long as he keeps us from God in the present moment, he is contented. He knows that by the time the future moments intended for God come, he can suggest some other use for them. His work is to suggest excuses why we should not meet God now — to suggest that we shall give our attention not to God but to our tired bodies, our aching head, our need for rest.

Still another difficulty lies in our natural proneness to seek rest, to stop growing. But in the spiritual life we either keep advancing or we regress. Never does any day come when God permits us to say, "This is enough." There must always be a daily increase. Yet how often the suggestions come to our minds, either from others or from our own self, that we take religion and praying in moderation, and that we must not be fanatical. But God is not content with anything less than all. He asks all; for he gives all. We learn unmistakably in Christian praying that we cannot belong to God and to ourselves. Never are we to presume that we are safe from sinning or that we have gone far enough toward God.

We pray, and we find that evil and unclean thoughts and desires come to us, even in the midst of our prayer. The Satanic thought comes to our mind, "If you were seeking God these evil thoughts would not come to you. Wait until you no longer have these evil thoughts, and then pray." Our hope and help in such times is to rest upon the foundation stone of God's loving holiness. It is because we are seeking God and his glory, and the salvation of our fellow men that these evil thoughts and desires come to us; Satan is using them to seek to divert us from God. We are to treat such thoughts and desires as we treat distractions. We turn immediately to God and the evil thoughts vanish. As oft as they return, so oft do we turn to God. We are to persevere in our turning to God. We know that the closer the saints came to God the more severe became the assaults of temptation. Those whom we call saints and whom we think to be free from evil thoughts and desires did not so think of themselves. So long as these evil thoughts and desires trouble us and something within us resists them, we are not to be anxious or troubled. All is going well. In fact, we are to take hope and be thankful, for our awareness of thoughts as evil is a sign that the spiritual warfare within us is continuing. So long as we continue to fight we are not defeated. We are on God's side.

The greatest danger of all is that we may fail to obey immediately and fully the inner promptings of the Indwelling Spirit. All of us know the many moments when a voice, not our own, suggests that we do an act. We all know also how easily and often we have disregarded this inner voice. We have tried to explain it away or to disobey it. We have pretended that it was not God's voice, but only our own. Then we could argue with it and disregard it. It is only by prompt and full obedience to this inner voice that we become sensitive to the pressure of God upon our lives, and thus give him the free consent of our wills to work his purposes in us. We need to watch over and heed every whisper which comes to us from that voice and never to act without his full consent.

Our only hope for perseverance through all obstacles lies in living fully and truly the whole life of Christian praying — adoration, self-giving, intercession, thankfulness. Unless we persevere, God is not glorified in our life, and moreover, since God has ordered that the salvation of each man is indissolubly linked up with the salvation of his fellow men, our perseverance may be the only hope of our fellow men being saved. For the sake of God's glory, and for the sake of our fellow men, we entreat God's Christ to give us this holy gift of perseverance.

O Lord God:

For thy glory, and
For the sake of our fellow men;
Make us to persevere.

PART V

"For Their Sakes"

And for their sakes I sanctify myself, that they also might be sanctified through the truth. John 17:19.

When we have learned to pray, to adore, to give ourselves to God wholly and unconditionally, to intercede, to be truly thankful; when we have nourished that life of praying by regular devotional reading; when we have entered into the wondrous joy of those who learn ever more deeply the secret of victory over temptation and sin; and persevere unto God: then there is born of God our Father in our praying a mighty missionary imperative — "For Their Sakes." We live in prayer unto God, not for ourselves, but for his people. We seek under the prevenience and providence of God to be a witness to others of the joyous fellowship with the Father, which comes in praying. Spontaneously and joyfully we offer our lives to God and accept those disciplines born of Christian love, which will ensure that others may, through our lives, be called to enter and live ever more deeply in the life of distinctively Christian praying.

15

The Retreat

WHEN WE HAVE entered fully and deeply into the life of Christian praying — adoration, self-giving, intercession, thankfulness — and through them have come to live for God, for his glory, and to have intimate and joyful companionship with God, our Father, we feel an inner impulsion born we know of the Indwelling Spirit, which drives us eagerly and spontaneously to desire that our fellow men, still imprisoned in the misery of self-centered living, may also enter into the perfect spiritual joy and freedom of the sons of God. We want them to enter into the life of prayer and to know God. How can we assure that they too shall enter into the life of Christian praying: recognize the basic foundations for such praying, and learn how to pray? Those of us who have attended retreats believe that they can be used as a unique channel to instruct men in beginning the life of Christian praying. With a wise and experienced man of prayer leading the retreat, it would provide a unique and perfect framework for teaching Christian praying.

Many people are not familiar with retreats, or have only misconceptions concerning them. They may have heard the term used, but never having attended a real retreat, they know not what are its purposes, its nature, and its methods. Some people object to the very word "retreat" as being an inept term, but such complaints usually come from people who have never attended them; those of us who have like the term.

The retreat is literally and frankly a "retreat," a withdrawing from the life of the world, as that life is commonly lived apart from, indifferent, or hostile to God; and thereby going apart for a period of days to live wholly and unconditionally unto God, living intimately with him, hearing no other words than his words, aware of no other presence but his presence. In the retreat we drop every other concern and give our whole and undivided attention to God. But it is not in any way a permanent flight from the world and men. It is rather a temporary "retreat" to take our spiritual bearings, and then we go back into the world again, with the light of God in our eyes, with deeper vision concerning the real needs of men and God's remedy for those needs; with deeper compassion and understanding for the sins of men and of the good tidings which God would have us bring to them from him.

The principle of the retreat is a very old one.

Jesus himself saw the need, both for himself and for his disciples, for withdrawing from the bustle and confusion and press of the crowds of Capernaum, and said to his disciples: "Come ye yourselves apart into a desert place and rest a while."

Concerned that others too shall learn to pray, and remembering our need in past years to be taught how to pray, we ourselves undertake the initiative of arranging for a retreat, having as its purpose that men shall be given instruction in Christian praying and shall be led to give and commit themselves to the life of praying. For our concern for these our fellow men is not simply that they shall have knowledge about praying, but that they shall be led to enter the life of prayer. We know that the retreat affords the perfect framework for both the learning of and the commitment to praying.

We know persons — acquaintances, business associates, friends — who do not know God, and whose lives are spiritually lonely, however much they seek to hide it from themselves or from us. We take the initiative — and behind our initiative lies the mighty initiative of God — of asking them, "We are planning to hold a retreat to teach men how to pray. Would you not like to come with us and learn from a man of prayer more of the wondrous and intimate friendship with God which prayer can give you?" We can surely find some who will grasp at such an opportunity as a drowning man grasps at straws. Thousands of men and women are hungrily waiting for us to take the initiative, for they are shy about asking for spiritual help.

We are constantly alert for some man or woman of prayer to lead retreats for our friends. As we seek, we shall find a suitable leader, for God himself will direct our searching; for he, far more than we, is seeking to lead men into that life with him which comes through prayer. God himself will crown our endeavors. We may have to search far and wide, but God has his hidden remnant who pray and who can teach others to pray. Even though we have to search far and go to some expense we are not to hesitate. What is at stake is not a few dollars, but the friendship which these our friends may have with God through a retreat on praying. If we are utterly unable to secure any leader, it may be God's way of leading us ourselves to undertake the work of teaching our friends how to pray.

We can usually find a place appropriate for a retreat — some country home or estate, available by auto or train, to which we can go. A summer home in the country, with extensive grounds, with woods and meadows, or water — lake, river, or sea — makes an ideal place for the retreat. It provides quiet and the vista of the wondrous handiwork of

God himself, and freedom from constant interruptions of people coming and going, of the ring of doorbell and telephone, of the rush and noise of traffic which dominate city life.

Having secured both a conductor and a place to hold the retreat all of us then gather there. We plan to arrive late in an afternoon, so that we all can get settled in our rooms before supper, when the retreat begins. Also by arriving early, we become acquainted with the house and grounds where we are to live for the next few days.

The retreat begins with supper — with table fellowship. We know that all have come here with a common purpose. All want to learn about praying. That is why they are there. That one common need at once links our lives together. It may be a very small group — five or six persons besides ourselves and the conductor. Or, if a number of us have planned together to hold the retreat, and each of us has brought four or five of our friends with us, then there may be twenty-five or more in attendance. At supper we all meet each other easily and effortlessly, for we are already brothers in our common need to learn to pray.

After an interval following supper, the conductor gathers us all together in a "common room," or if it is an established retreat house, in the chapel. There he leads us in Evening Prayer, immediately after which he gives us the opening instruction of the retreat. He as leader will be an experienced retreat conductor. He is a man of God, and therefore a man of prayer. He knows deeply and authoritatively the foundations of Christian praying and the purposes of God in that life, and of man's deep spiritual needs and of man's deep resistances to God. It is of these matters that he will give us instruction in the subsequent sessions. But in this first session he will remind us why we have come into retreat. We have come to learn how to pray, to receive teaching about praying, and to give ourselves to God to live the life of praying. We have not come to the retreat merely in order to have a pleasant week-end in the country, nor to escape from the city, nor to get a much-needed rest. We have come in order to be with God, and to be taught of him in and through praying.

The conductor will explain to us the use of silence, for beginning with the opening session, we all enter upon the discipline of silence, understanding that until the final meal of the retreat we are to speak to nobody. Probably few of those attending the retreat are familiar with silence over prolonged periods. The conductor will realize our unfamiliarity and will therefore explain to us the purpose and use of silence. Silence is a means to an end, not an end in itself. Its goal is that through silence we shall become stilled — externally and within — and thus be prepared to meet God and to be enabled to hear the whisper of his voice within our minds and hearts — that voice which we must learn to hear and to heed. Few of us are at ease in silence. Our busy and noisy world does not train us for it. Often we are afraid of silence, and know not what to do with it, or in it. We refrain from talking in retreat because we do not want to consider superficial and secular things, and much of our talking is superficial and trivial. Often talking is escape from being alone with our own thoughts, and escape from facing God and listening to the Indwelling Spirit.

But more than exterior silence is required if we are truly to keep the retreat. Even though our lips may be stilled, the mind and inner life may still be in very much confusion and turmoil. The conductor will counsel us to quiet the inner life by quietly dropping each thought and desire as it comes into our minds, and by deliberately turning our attention toward God. We drop each secular thought one by one, replacing each rejected one by another directed to God, and slowly we shall find that we become peacefully stilled in our inner being. In that inner stillness we shall be met by the prevenient God. The conductor will have told us that our coming to the retreat has been the result of the hidden, prevenient leading of God, however unbeknown to us. God is seeking us in the retreat; it is upon the foundation of his seeking that we place our hope and trust, and not upon that of our seeking God. We seek God only because he has first been seeking us.

All during the retreat we are to seek to keep stilled within and to pay humble and obedient attention to every dim stirring that comes to the inner life. When thoughts come to us from God they have a note of authority to them, which is not true of the thoughts which have their origin in our own self. In the retreat we learn to distinguish between the thoughts that come from God and all others. God's thoughts bring us peace, not restlessness; they never argue with us; they command us with the entreaty of love; we have power to say "No" or to say "Yes," but we know we have no power to change the word which comes from God.

After a time we welcome the prolonged silence. There is a peace in that silence which we have never before known. We know that in the silence God is our unseen, invisible companion, as we sit in the chapel, or as we walk in the woods, or as we eat; God is ever present with us at each moment. And his presence brings us spiritual joy through judgment and cleansing. We gain a new knowledge of ourselves as we walk with him, and it is a knowledge which sets us free from our miserable self-centeredness. We are gaining insight into a new kind of life — a life which is lived with God at the center.

There come times of course when distractions lead us from God, but as often as they come, so often do we quietly drop them and turn back again to God. We persevere in turning back to God again and again.

In this first instruction the conductor will teach us these things, and following his counsel we shall be able to enter into the purpose and discipline of the retreat, and be able to recognize the experiences as they come to us from hour to hour.

At about nine o'clock we all gather together again in the chapel and the conductor leads us in prayers, after which we retire for the night.

At about seven-thirty the next morning we again gather in the chapel for a service of the Holy Communion, or other morning devotions. At breakfast which follows, while we eat, the conductor reads to us from some spiritual biography, religious play, or book of spiritual letters. Such reading is to help us to keep under the discipline of silence, and to keep ever before us the constant remembrance of God. Often we find that some word or words in this reading at mealtimes strikes a response in us. We are to heed such thoughts, and ponder them. Initial awkwardness at this practice of reading at meals soon passes away, and we come to feel a deep peace and spiritual joy at not having to carry on "table talk."

During the day, perhaps at ten o'clock in the

morning, at three-thirty in the afternoon, and in the evening at eight o'clock, we listen humbly and receptively to the conductor's instructions in praying. We find it helps to take notes so that we shall not forget. Then in the silences after the instructions we look over our notes, think and pray over the matters the conductor has been teaching us, and start to practice the praying he has taught us.

If the conductor is to give us at all adequate instruction in Christian praying, he will need six such periods. In these six instructions he can then give us teaching in adoration, self-giving, intercession, thankfulness, devotional reading, and perseverance, and work into these instructions some of the basic foundation teaching concerning Christian praying. Teaching such as is contained in this book can be used for such a retreat. If the retreat begins on a Friday evening at supper, then by continuing all day Saturday and Sunday, six teaching sessions are provided, and the retreat may close either after the last Sunday-evening instruction or on Monday morning after breakfast.

The real test of the worth of the retreat is that it works; it leads men into the life of Christian praying. The teaching given in the framework of the retreat reaches the retreatants as they are in the mood of quietude, receptiveness, expectancy, humility. The retreatant then spends many hours in the silence attentive to God, ever more deeply aware of the presence and action of God in and upon him. The retreatant feels within him the necessity for commitment to the life of prayer. Knowledge about praying must pass over into actual living of the life of praying. And the retreatant can go out into the life of the world, with the call to live under worldly conditions the Christian life of praying. In retreat he has received the vision of what the life of prayer can be; he has been given wise and practical instruction in praying; he has lived for these days of retreat in the companionship of God and with fellow men who likewise are seeking to learn to pray. He has become an integral part of the Christian fellowship. Having made this initial commitment, he now knows where he may turn for further help and spiritual companionship. He wants to pray and turns constantly to God to give him perseverance in praying. Over the years another man has been led into the great fellowship with God which comes from prayer.

16

The School of Prayer

AS EARNEST CHRISTIANS, living in Christian praying, we accept the great missionary imperative, born of the Indwelling Spirit, to call our fellow men into the joyous, spiritual freedom and power of the life of prayer, which leads us into rich and wondrous fellowship with God, and also with our fellow men. We yearn and hunger that our fellow men shall know God as it has been given to us to know him. We do not want them to miss God.

In addition to using the retreat as a method of inviting some of our fellow men to enter the life of praying, we want also to use another available method to reach men with the good tidings of the life of prayer. We realize that there are many who will never be able to attend a retreat: the demands of home, children, and aged ones to care for make it impossible; not all can give the time required. But there is a method, which can offer to all people the opportunity of learning to pray — the school of prayer. Some people learn best not by reading a book, but by hearing a person teach, catching from him by contagion his teaching and life. A school of prayer offers men a fellowship in learning to pray, when if left to themselves, they would do nothing about it. Many learn best by learning together. We who have shared in a school of prayer know its power to reach large numbers of people with this much needed teaching; and we also know that schools of prayer have borne rich fruit in actually leading people to undertake the life of praying as a means toward greater spiritual living.

Where schools of prayer have been offered there has been a very real response, both on the part of clergy and laity. It meets a real need in men's lives, and we have faith and hope that were the school of prayer used more widely it would reach many spiritually hungry people and that it would lead many of them into the life of praying, and through that into new and deeper fellowship with God.

How do we go about arranging for a school of prayer? As clergymen, concerned deeply that our people, entrusted to us by God, shall be taught and led into truly Christian praying, we can ourselves take the initiative. Either we can suggest to our parish council or vestry the holding of a parish school of prayer; or we can consult with our fellow clergy in the community about holding an interdenominational or community school of prayer. When we deal with prayer, we are dealing with that which is so central and important to those of every church that we can well do this work corporately. The life of true Christian praying is uniquely free from denominational bias. It compels us to deal with basic realities which are common to all church traditions. The laws are the same for all, and the methods for the most part identical. One of the deepest and surest means of bringing about a deeper understanding of universal Christian truths, and through them of entering into a more Christian unity of purpose and action, is that of praying. When Christians become truly praying Christians, many of our denominational differences will evaporate and will no longer constitute dividing barriers; we shall become united in Christian praying.

If we are planning to hold an interdenominational or community school of prayer, the first immediate need is to secure an adequate leader. There are not many persons now available to lead such schools, but as demand increases God will supply them. People must learn to pray — that is all-important; and because it is so important we are to ascertain God's prevenient purposes and then use our utmost ingenuity to secure an adequate leader.

When the leader comes from a distance, that factor alone in large measure determines the set-up of the school: a minimum of six sessions is required to give sufficient instruction to the people; it may involve arranging the school for six successive evenings, an hour for each session. If the leader is secured from a near-by place, the school may be planned either to run over six successive evenings, or to be extended over a period of six successive weeks, one hour each week. Each plan has its special advantages. The school completed in one week serves to give a comprehensive picture of prayer in a short time, so that the people attending are enabled to see the relation of each kind of praying to all the others very quickly. The extended school of prayer has the advantage of enabling the people to practice each type of praying for a week, before receiving instruction in the next kind of praying. It makes more possible the combination of instruction and practice.

When one of us clergymen has enlarged and deepened his own life of praying and thus has become a man of prayer, he holds a school of prayer for his parish people. He gives an extended series of Sunday-morning sermon hours to teaching his people more about prayer. Or he can use a weekday evening over a period of weeks to hold a school of prayer in a more informal setting than that of the Sunday-morning hour of corporate worship. Where a minister does this for his own people, it establishes a deep, spiritual fellowship between himself and them, and between them all and God. Each of these three types of school will bring to many new life with God.

In any case, the leader of the school, if he is to teach and interpret the life of praying with convincing ability and authority, must be himself a man of devotion, one who has lived for years under the disciplines of Christian praying. His people will sense instinctively and accurately whether or not he is speaking with the ability and authority on these matters which are born out of long experience in praying.

Whatever the type of school held, it is necessary to make extensive, careful, and long-range preparations for it over several months. People must be informed of the dates, so that they can arrange to clear from all other engagements the six consecutive evenings of one week or the one day in six consecutive weeks. Then publicity to the school can be given in the local papers and in the weekly church bulletins. Prayers on behalf of the school — both for the leader and those attending — are offered to God in each church at every service of worship. Individuals who plan to attend can be given a printed prayer card, and be asked to pray daily for the school. They can be asked to tell their friends and neighbors about it and to urge them to attend.

The leader of the school will be daily offering himself to God on behalf of the people who will attend. With his praying for the people, and their praying for him, when the school actually begins a bond of spiritual fellowship has already been born of God. We shall be more humble and receptive as we sit before him to be taught how to pray.

The school sessions can be held either in the church itself or in the parish hall. When held in the church itself, they will have the added help of all the devotional associations of years of worship. The sense of awe which comes from being in a place never used for any other purpose than the worship of God will also help. But whether held in the church or in the parish hall, the school sessions need to be simple and informal. No choirs are needed.

The leader seats himself in front, close to the people. Sitting there, rather than giving instruction from the pulpit or reading desk, a note of quiet repose comes over the sessions. Standing is the posture for oratory. Sitting is the ancient posture for a teacher. The leader begins each session by a few simple, short prayers, invoking God's help and blessing. A quiet, simple hymn may be sung. Then the leader is seated and gives the instructions. He must not read a lecture from a manuscript. The fewer his notes, the better. The most effective teaching is spoken from the heart.

The leader is always ready and glad to answer questions at the end of each session, and often small groups of individuals remain for some time, gaining through the give and take of informal questioning an even deeper understanding of the teaching as it is presented in varying forms. Often we fully grasp a new teaching only after it has been presented to us in different ways. Just as in music, we find our enjoyment enhanced by our recognition of the basic motive after it has been repeated in new dress, so too with the basic teachings concerning prayer, we begin to make them our own only after they have been repeatedly offered to us in many different forms.

Over the six sessions the leader gives the teaching contained in the chapters of this book: "Adoration," "Self-Giving," "Intercession," "Thankfulness," "Devotional Reading," "Perseverance." At the final session it has often been found helpful to make practical suggestions about the follow-up of the school. The purpose of the school is not simply to provide instruction, but also to make a repeated appeal to those attending it to give themselves to the life of praying. Each night's session ends with the leader using a prayer, which expresses this self-giving to God. And on the final night there is a period of silence in which each person is asked to dedicate himself to God that he may enter into actual praying as a life vocation. Opportunity is offered for those so desiring to hand in their names for the purpose of forming small prayer cells. Individuals are encouraged to form the practice of going into the quiet church during the week for a few moments of prayer; thus making the church more truly a house of prayer. Intercessory prayer cells can be formed. Good books concerning the spiritual life can be obtained and made available to the people, either in the public library on a special shelf of devotional books or in the church libraries.

Much of the fruit of a school of prayer will be invisible, known only to the all-seeing God and to individual persons. It is not at all necessary that all that happens should be publicized. If even a few people, if only one person is led into a saving fellowship with God, the school has been blessed of God. It is definitely known that many have been richly blessed and led into prayer through going to schools of prayer.

Those of us who are clergymen have a deep and serious responsibility to provide for the people of our communities — not simply for those formally listed as members of our own churches. Part of this responsibility is to provide for them retreats and schools of prayer. We are not to rest content or to be at ease until we have held them again and again. Through them people who know little or nothing about praying can truly be awakened and led into the life of praying, and so into saving fellowship with God. The retreat for prayer and the school of prayer are primarily for those who know little or nothing of praying, to offer them elemental instruction in praying and to call them into praying. But we also are concerned that those who already pray, and who have had this elemental instruction, shall grow in the life of praying, and we need therefore to concern ourselves with their needs. How can we help them to grow in praying, and to penetrate ever more deeply into the life of praying, and so into ever-deepening fellowship with God?

17

The Layman's Life of Praying

AFTER WE AS laymen have received the basic teachings in praying, whether it be from a book, or from the teaching received in a retreat or a school of prayer we find ourselves confronted with a further need. How can we be helped to keep our praying from becoming intermittent and haphazard? Our intentions may be perfect; we intend to continue faithfully at prayer. Our spirit is willing, but our flesh is weak. We soon realize that the life of praying is too important to leave to the mercy of whim, feeling, desire, or even of will, because our wills are still weak. We need the reinforcement of a help that lies outside ourselves. We are the reality that requires to be changed. Therefore we cannot depend upon our own wills, even at their best. So easy is it to ignore and pay no heed to the whisperings of the Indwelling Spirit.

Some of us have been led under God's wise providence to obey the suggestion, which we know came from him, to place our lives under the discipline of a rule of praying. Even after a short time we came to realize the indispensable aid of this help. In times of discouragement and despair, of fatigue and weariness, when if left to our own wills we would have omitted or abandoned praying, we felt the strength of a rule of prayer come to our rescue to carry our weak wills over the time of danger. A power not our own — a will stronger than our own will — came to us and steadied our wavering decisions, and gave us the motivation to continue steadfastly. How thankful we are to God for the support of a rule of prayer at such times.

A rule of prayer is for us a means to an end, and not an end in itself. We place our lives under a rule of prayer to make sure that we do the actual praying, which we know we ought to do. The rule reminds us of the deep foundations of our praying. It calls us back from surface living to the deep, firm, abiding center of life — God. It is a discipline under which we have voluntarily placed ourselves, so that we may be reminded of the purposes of praying in times when they have become dimmed and vague. The rule of prayer is rooted and grounded in the will of the prevenient Creator, the redeeming, indwelling God; it is rooted in the law of creation — that we are made for God, for his glory, for intimate fellowship with him, and for spiritual fellowship with our fellow creatures.

The rule is rooted in the goal of growing up into that perfect freedom of the sons of God in which we shall have but one will — to do the will of our Father. It is rooted too in our calling from God to grow up into the unselfish loving of God for his own sake, that loving life in which we seek not our own, but only God's glory and the blessing and salvation of our fellow men. In all of these deep, central truths the rule of prayer is rooted. Therefore, in times of indecision and wavering and temptation to turn from God and live for ourselves, the mighty energies of God which operate in and upon us through these truths come to support and strengthen us, giving us endurance and perseverance to turn immediately back to God.

When we have read and accepted the basic teaching in praying which has been given to us in a book such as this, or which we have received in a retreat for praying, or from a school of prayer, we know that we ought to adore God daily; to give ourselves wholly and unconditionally to God each day, ever pressing into deeper levels of Christian self-giving; to intercede for our fellow creatures, unselfishly offering all that we are and all that we have to God for their sakes; to be thankful for all that each day holds, knowing day by day ever more deeply the wise and loving initiative and providence of God; to give some time each day to planting in our lives the creative word-seeds of God that they may germinate and grow in us; to persevere against the obstacles that come to us daily, by turning back repeatedly and immediately to God.

We want to implement this general desire to do all of this by giving it definite embodiment in definite ways. We do this by humbly and prayerfully going into the presence of God and seeking to know and to follow his will in these matters. We write down the rule of praying which we believe will carry out the teaching which we have accepted. Each day we determine to be an adorer; on waking, repeatedly throughout the day, and as the last act of the day. Each morning early in the day, we will make a rule to give ourselves wholly and unconditionally to God. We will set aside definite times each day — for example, fifteen minutes at noon, and by going into a particular church where we can be quiet and undisturbed — for the work of interceding for those particular people whom God means us to carry in praying. We shall pray for them day after day. We shall set aside twenty minutes — for example, on the train going to or returning from work, or the time directly before beginning the household chores of the day — for reading in the Bible and some particular classic of devotion. Each Sunday we determine, so far as circumstances under our control permit, to worship God in his church, and determine to arrange every other plan for Sunday to fit in with this central and primary purpose of the day to honor God.

We write out all of this as our rule of praying,

in the presence of God, offering our lives to God to observe it. Then we seek out some person whom we love and respect for his deep and stable spirituality and ask him to check us from time to time on our observance of this rule. We need him to do this for us. We all have had much experience with good resolutions which we have made and which we have never followed. There is a wide gulf between our resolutions and our observance of them. Self is never the person to examine self. We need the firmness of an external examination if we are to face ourselves. Asking our minister to check us up once each month, or more frequently, is a wise procedure, and will lead us to have a deeper kind of spiritual relation with him. Or we can make use of some mature and wise layman. The realization that each month we must be examined by another person as to our observance of our rule of praying is a great source of incentive to do the acts of praying. Having to acknowledge our failures serves to make us more humble and more dependent upon the patient and unfailing grace of God. We gain deeper and deeper self-knowledge through our failures; and a deeper and deeper sense of thankfulness to God for our successes. And from it all we grow into the practice of regular and faithful praying, and through such regularity we enter into deeper and firmer fellowship with God, and so the central purpose of the rule is fulfilled.

18

The Minister's Life of Praying

THOSE OF US who have been called by God into the work of the Christian ministry must be truly and wholly men of God, men who belong undividedly and unswervingly to God, and are therefore set free from self-seeking in all its myriad and subtle forms. We are to be men who voluntarily have surrendered ourselves — all that we are and all that we have — to the sovereignty of God. Into our care God has committed the lives of certain of his people, that we may, under his providence, call them, teach them, and lead them into saving fellowship with himself, in order that God's purposes for their lives may be fulfilled. In a special way, therefore, because of our acceptance and commitment to the vocation of the Christian ministry, we clergy must be men of prayer. We dare not attempt to do his work without the preparation and dedication of praying. We cannot belong to ourselves; for the sake of his people we must belong to God — wholly, unconditionally, forever and ever.

Our life of praying therefore must be rooted in a holy and loving discipline — a discipline gladly and voluntarily entered into and unswervingly obeyed — in order that out of our disciplined life of praying we may fulfill God's purpose for our ministries to his people; that we may be authoritative guides and counsellors in those matters which pertain to God and his salvation of the people committed to our charge and care. We have but one will (in our ministries for his people) : that they, one by one, shall ever more and more truly and deeply know, love, and obey God. That they may accomplish this, we must call them into the life of Christian praying, teach them how to pray, and counsel them to nourish that life of prayer and to persevere in it unto the end. We know that God wills them to enter into the life of adoration, self-giving, intercession, thankfulness; and to nourish their praying upon devotional reading regularly and lovingly done. But we have no authority to call them into the life of praying, if we ourselves do not live in that life. We dare not call others or teach them to pray, if we ourselves do not pray. For their sakes, we turn to God and give ourselves wholly and unconditionally and forever to the life of praying. But that means that we dare not root our praying in occasion and circumstance, in mood or need, and not even in our own wills. We root our praying in God and in his will for us and our ministries to his people. We know that we need to place our praying under a rule of praying.

Under existing church conditions it is not easy for us to be men of prayer. There are many obstacles to face, but if we turn to God, he will reveal to us the ways and means by which we can truly become men of prayer. The obstacles are not insurmountable if we turn to God for guidance. God wills us to be men of prayer. Therefore we can, and under God we will, be men of prayer.

Our first immediate problem is to secure a prolonged period of uninterrupted time daily in which to do this praying, in which we can give ourselves to God, and do our devotional reading. For when we give ourselves lovingly and obediently to God, we find that we are given the holy and saving wisdom of God himself to be victorious over temptation and sin in our own lives and so to become truer and more helpful spiritual counsellors to his people in their inner warfare. The perseverance in praying which is rooted in God, and not simply in our own weak wills, makes us more faithful interpreters of God and man to our people.

Already our days are too full of too many peripheral activities, and the central, weighty matters of the real purpose of our ministries — that our people live for God's glory and have fellowship with God — get pushed aside. At first sight it may seem a stark impossibility to find and to keep an extended period of time in which to be alone with God. But God wants us to have time each day in which we shall be with him and with him alone, that he may make us ever more truly and deeply his ministers. It is he, and not we, who takes the initiative in this matter of entering into the life of prayer. Often he has intimated to us the impotency of our activities which are not rooted in praying; again and again we are reminded, as we reread the words of our ordination service, or attend the ordination of some clergyman, of the awful responsibility which is ours as a shepherd of God's sheep; God presses us from without in his providence and from within by his Indwelling Spirit, offering to us the will to pray. God calls us to prayer. Dare we give him any reply but "Yes"? God wills it; therefore in loving obedience we will give him the time he asks of us for praying. We will make time for him every day.

We need at least a full hour each morning of absolutely uninterrupted time, in which we can give our loving attention exclusively and undividedly to him. For most of us there is probably only one time of the day when we can be fully assured of having a full hour free from all interruptions. That time is early dawn. We remember that Jesus "rising up a great while before day . . . went out, and departed into a solitary place, and there prayed."

If he needed that time in prayer with his Father, in order to do his Father's will in his ministry, how much more do we need it. Before wife and children have awakened, and before the active life of the household has begun for the day, we too can rise up "a great while before day," and pray. It is a time when the telephone and doorbell do not ring. Many of our parish people are still in bed, and there is little likelihood of our people making demands upon our time at that hour. Unbroken time then — an hour as a minimum — is worth twice that amount of time later in the day, when there are almost certain to be interruptions.

In the beginning we shall probably require the aid of strong discipline, rooted in unselfish love for God and for our people, to get us up and out of bed and to our praying. We shall need the deep and abiding conviction that God wants us to rise and pray; and that it is God himself who awakens us each morning and calls us to rise and pray. Because God wants it, and because without praying we cannot meet or even know the real spiritual needs of his people, and because if we fail them in this matter of praying they may perish eternally — therefore we find ourselves gladly, willingly, lovingly, obediently rising early and praying. When we have these early morning hours with God in praying there come into our lives a spiritual joy and peace which pass all human understanding. No other joy or peace given by the world even compares with this spiritual joy and peace of God. We find that our days and our ministries to his people become very different, because of these early hours at dawn with God. We can and do rise and pray if we are truly dedicated to the doing of God's will. If we are still only half-committed to his will and to his work, and are secretly seeking to do our own will and to shape our own ministries, then of course we shall be able to find a thousand excuses why we need not, cannot, and do not rise early and pray. Are we in our ministries seeking to do our will or to do God's will? Do we belong to ourselves or do we belong to God? We must make a rule then of rising early for prayer. We are to make this rule specific and definite; not simply that some time during the day, if and when it is convenient to the world, we shall pray; but at this particular hour — six o'clock, five o'clock, or whatsoever other early hour each morning we may designate, led by God's guidance — we shall rise and pray.

Many of us have found great help and strength in spending this early morning hour for praying in the church. True, there are sections of this country where, because of climatic conditions, churches are unheated during the week in winter; but there are many of us who, because we are not faced with this difficulty, could use our churches for praying, and so help to make them more and more houses of prayer. Many of us live near enough to our churches so that we could, either by walking or driving, go to the church for this early morning hour of prayer. There we can be certain of not being interrupted in our praying. Moreover, praying there lends us all the aid which comes from a building dedicated exclusively to God and to his worship. All the imagery and associations of the building help us to attend to God. Where we cannot go to the church either because of distance or of cold, then we can have this early hour in our home, in our study or in some room set apart exclusively for a place of prayer — an oratory. We need a rule, stating definitely and specifically the place where we shall spend our early morning hour of praying. Not somewhere, sometime; but here, at this hour.

What shall we do in this early morning time devoted to praying? If we keep regularly this time for praying, God himself will gradually teach us the best use of it. Spontaneously we shall want to begin with adoration. We want to begin each new day by turning to the almighty, transcendent, prevenient, loving Father, God, asking nothing for ourselves, but concerned wholly with him. This unselfish adoration of God is the background for all of our praying. No other kind of praying gives such deep

THE MINISTER'S LIFE OF PRAYING 233

and abiding spiritual joy. We shall also want to dedicate, by an act of new and deeper self-giving, our whole being to God for his service this day. We want each morning to enter more deeply into renunciation of self-ownership, and belong each day more fully and perfectly to God. Only as we grow into this deeper "belonging to God" can we be set free from self-possessing and be able to be servants of God to his people. Adoration and self-giving will not take much actual clock time; their worth is measured not by the number of clock minutes they consume, but by how much of ourselves we put into their doing. Each morning in adoration and self-giving we partake in a new and deeper service of ordination. God himself ordains us each morning. Adoration and self-giving are our response to God's prevenience, seeking to make us more truly and deeply his ministers. We shall want to be sure, as part of our rule of praying, that each morning we begin the new day with an act of adoration and an act of self-giving.

Our early morning self-giving will spontaneously pass over into intercession for his people, whom he has committed to our loving care. In intercession, we take up the deep and loving concern that each one of these children of God shall enter into that fellowship with God for which he has created them. We give ourselves each morning to God for them, asking him to take all that we are and all that we have and to use it for the fulfillment of his redemptive will for these his people. We turn to God and give ourselves to him for them. We offer God our lives, so that through us he may enter into their lives. We offer our lives to God for them so that they may through us have understanding and fellowship with God. Whether one by one, or as groups, or as a parish family, we begin each day by turning to God and offering him our lives for their sakes.

When we give ourselves to Christian intercession, we notice that we enter into a new relationship with these people. We go to them during the day in our calling, ministering to them in sorrow and in joy, in sickness and in health, in light and in darkness — but going always not in our own name, but in the name of God. Not we, but God it is who helps them. We are but the channels of God's work. When our people know that we are truly men of God and that we begin each day by going apart with God to offer ourselves unselfishly and lovingly to God for them, they too will have very different relationships with us. The important matter is not one of techniques or words. The essential matter is that we hunger and thirst that each of the people entrusted to our spiritual care by God shall come to know him, to love him, to obey him, and to glorify him. Only godly love knows how to intercede.

This early morning hour, too, is the most apt and perfect time in which to do our daily devotional reading. When devotional reading becomes an integral part of this morning hour, we come to it in the mood already created by our prayers of adoration, self-giving, and intercession. In such reading we find ourselves adoring, giving ourselves again and again to God, and interceding anew for our people. Morning after morning we read devotionally in the Word of God — in the Bible and some chosen classic of devotion. Humbly, lovingly, receptively, we let God plant his words in the soil of our lives, to bring in future years the rich harvest that he will give us. Each morning, too, we reap the harvest from devotional reading done in past years.

From these early morning hours with God we go forth into the active life of each new day — into our own family life, into the needs and lives of our people, ever with the presence of God accompanying us in all that we do. Never for one moment does God leave us. Always in his prevenient love he seeks to guide us and direct us in the work that he would have us to do. Wherever we go, whatever we do, we are his workmen and his friends. We live and work by him, with him, and for him. We bring to our people not ourselves; we bring them God.

More and more of us are forming the additional

practice of going in the afternoon again into the church. It is too late to make house calls; committee meetings are over, and people are traveling homeward from their day's work; housewives are busy preparing for supper. We take advantage of these facts to go again into the quiet church and to be alone with God. Kneeling or sitting in the church we quietly and peacefully bring to God all that the day has held for us and for our people. We bring God his sheep that he may fold them for the night. We know that our people need not only our ministry to them, but God's never-ceasing ministry to them. All through the night hours, while we must sleep and rest, we know that he untiringly watches over them. This is our time to practice daily thankfulness to God. For out of our daily companionship with God there has been born the ever-deepening sense of God's loving providence over the lives of our people. For that providence which never faileth we turn to God and give him thanks, confident that he will gradually awaken us to all that he has done to us and to our people through the day.

We can also well use some of this time of the late afternoon for additional devotional reading. All through the day we have heard much of the words of the world. Now, at the close of day, we would hear again no words but the words of God, our Father. We know we cannot ever sufficiently feed upon his words. Without them, we cannot feed his people with those words which are the bread of life.

As Christian ministers we shall want to place this daily praying under the help of a wise and loving discipline, make up a definite rule of praying, particular and definite in every aspect of praying. And because we know how easily we are apt to escape deep and piercing examination, when we examine ourselves, we shall want to search out some wise and godly man — our bishop or superintendent — and ask him from time to time to check us on our observance of the rule we have made. Over the years we shall often give God thanks for the aid and strength of such a rule of praying, and know that without it we often would have utterly failed both God and his people in our ministries.

* * * * *

"For their sakes" — that is to be the mood of our life of praying. Day by day, year after year, our concern for our fellow men grows deeper and deeper, more truly Christian. We want to use the retreat, and the school of prayer, and every other method we can find to make sure that the people whom God is seeking to lead into the life of prayer actually learn to pray and do pray. For their sakes, too, we place our individual lives — whether we be clergy or laity — under the wise discipline of a rule of praying. Only so can those who know not God, in seeing our lives, find there those marks which are the evidences that we have been much with God — spiritual love, joy, peace, power. And more and more our concern will reach out to that great multitude of men in every class of society, in every nation, and of every race who have never yet known God and his joyous fellowship. We see them living in the world without God, living in darkness, joylessness, hungering and thirsting, although they know it not, for spiritual fellowship with God. We see the world and all its many social problems, and we know that the only power and light which can solve these problems is that which is given to man as he enters into and participates fully in the Christian life of praying.

PART VI

"Except Ye Be Converted"

ἐπιστρέψον — μετανοῆσον
turn — change your mind

19

Praying and Social Issues

HERE IS THE TIME and the place in this "Study of Distinctively Christian Praying" to teach the effective power of the life of Christian praying on social issues. Not at all has the author been insensitive to or unaware of pressing social problems and needs, but he holds a very deep conviction, born of many years of praying: *social issues can be dealt with adequately only at the level of individual conversion.* When our Lord came to man to save him, he did not engage directly in social welfare work, or attack directly the social structure of existing society. Instead he gave himself to the task of converting, remaking, and training twelve apparently unimportant men. Dare *we* follow in the footsteps of his holy wisdom?

The heart of any social problem lies in the heart of individual men and women. New social structures and systems, new laws, can never solve the problem, so long as the heart of man remains selfish. Only when men, one by one, pass over by conversion from self-centeredness to God-centeredness can we achieve a social structure which will be truly acceptable to all classes, all nations, and all races. Granted that the prayers of any individual, important or unimportant, have no quick and easy and immediate effect upon the structure of our society, which is still so predominantly pagan, yet in the long run prayer has the greatest and the only effective power to change society, for the heart of the problem is the cleansing of the heart of man, the humbling of his proud intellect, and the surrender and dedication of his will to the will of God.

All of our external social problems — e.g. race, nationalism, war, economics, politics, power — all of these are but the external symptoms of an internal, deep-seated disease — the sin of self-centeredness. The only strategy which will be victorious in the warfare against social problems is an offensive directed not against a class, a nation, or a race, but against the individual. The point of attack is the self-centeredness of the individual man. The objective of attack is the conversion of the individual man.

Only when individual men give themselves to the full life of distinctively Christian praying — to adoration, self-giving, intercession, thankfulness; only when they are unceasingly nourished by God in that life of prayer and persevere against all obstacles, turning ever to him in holy and loving obedience; only when that life of prayer is rooted firmly in the distinctive Christian conviction that the Creator, Redeemer God is ever taking the initiative, coming to man to dwell in him, bringing to man an awakening to his deep sinfulness, and bringing also the cleansing power of God's own sinlessness, leading man into the perfect freedom of the sons of God, awakening man to the mighty wonder of God's own unselfish love; only then can individual men, classes, nations, and races be set free from the misery and tragedy of their self-seeking, and enter into that new life in which all men, classes, nations, and races will live for God and for his glory and have ever-deepening fellowship with God, and because of that fellowship with him have *Christian* brotherhood with one another — only then can they fulfill the will of God.

O GOD,
make us perfect in praying to do thy will,
working in us that which is well-pleasing in
thy sight;
for thou art the God who art able to do
exceedingly abundantly
above all that we ask or think.

www.ingramcontent.com/pod-product-compliance
Lightning Source LLC
Chambersburg PA
CBHW050845230426
43667CB00012B/2161